MW01633990

They're YOUR Kids

A Personal Journey From Self-Doubter to Home School Advocate

Mrs. Sam Sorbo

Reveille Press

Other books by Sam Sorbo

Gizmoe: The Legendary Journeys, Auckland

The Answer: Proof of God in Heaven

They're Your Kids

Cover design by PixelStudio
Interior images are my own unless otherwise indicated.

Published by Reveille Press

ISBN: 978-0-9828001-0-2

First Printing: April 2016

Printed in the United States of America

First Edition: April 2016

WITH THANKS TO GOD.

For my children,
and for yours.

ACKNOWLEDGEMENTS

If I had never had children, of course, I never would have thought to write this book. I am especially grateful to Braeden, Shane and Octavia for presenting me with the tremendous opportunity to share my life with them. Home schooling is an extraordinary journey. We are taking it together, and they are educating me as much or more than I teach them.

This book would never have happened without the gentle insistence of my sister, Joryn, and the indulgence and encouragement of my husband, Kevin.

I am extremely grateful for the insights of other home schoolers and the support of the home school community, a gathering of truly liberal-minded people who simply love children and respect education. We are blessed to live in an incredible country that affords us the freedom to do both.

What Others Are Saying About This Book...

~

"Sam Sorbo is one of the most brilliant and wise Christian media voices. Whatever she says and writes is must listen and read. I highly recommend her."

— Ted Beahr, Founder and Publisher of MOVIEGUIDE®

"Interesting and entertaining! Sam explains why home education is necessary while realistically demonstrating how to succeed. Her easy approach and striking insights make this book a necessity for devoted parents."

— Colin Gunn, award-winning writer/director/producer, *IndoctriNation: Public Schools and the Decline of Christianity in America*

"Finally, a book that thinks like I do! Who decides the child's values, morals, culture and principles? The teacher does. If you compromise on principles you won't have any. Public education is child abuse. God gave your children to you, for you to pass on your wisdom, not for you to outsource their indoctrination. Sam's book will give you the insights you need to make this courageous and consequential choice, and the resources and understanding to succeed."

— Mason Weaver, author, *It's Okay to Leave the Plantation* and *Tribalism*

"Loving parents commonly tell their children to do all sorts of simple matter-of-fact things, like "eat your veggies," "do you homework" and "pick up your room." In her fascinating new book, Sam Sorbo has a simple and common sense message to those same parents: teach your children, show them you are committed to their future success, and please don't outsource their training to strangers who have pledged allegiance to a system bent on alienating your children from you and your values by indoctrinating them with a socialist worldview. I encourage you to read Sam's compelling story, examine your priorities and take her life-changing challenge."

— Joaquin Fernandez, filmmaker, *IndoctriNation: Public Schools and the Decline of Christianity in America*

"Sam Sorbo examines the state of public education and obeys God's command to "train up a child in the way he should go." In particular, when she is confronted with pornography in the literature, and sees how Common Core is meant to produce anti-God, sexually promiscuous slaves of the state (Brave New World) she does the right thing and home schools. As a former radical, liberal atheist existentialist I too saw the toxicity the progressive Marxists had created for our children when I served President Reagan as his appointee to America 2000, which was the forerunner of Common Core. Read this personal journey and join Sam in saving our children!"

— Donna Hearne, Reagan Official 1981-1989.

TABLE OF CONTENTS

"Education should aim at destroying free will so that after pupils are thus schooled they will be incapable throughout the rest of their lives of thinking or acting otherwise than as their school masters would have wished... When the technique has been perfected, every government that has been in charge of education for more than one generation will be able to control its subjects securely without the need of armies or policemen."

~ Bertrand Russell, quoting Johann Gottlieb Fichte, the head of philosophy & psychology at Prussian University in Berlin, who influenced the entire public school movement.

FORWARD

By Curtis Bowers

~

I have been blessed with many unique opportunities in my life. I've traveled to all 50 states, and have many fond memories in each. I've been blessed with an incredible wife for 27 years, and God has given us 9 fantastic children. I've started three different restaurants in three different cities and each received numerous "Best Restaurant" awards. I've had the unique experience of receiving a call from the governor of my state asking me to be the new representative for my district. And incredibly, God blessed the very first film I ever made by allowing it to win the largest single cash prize film festival in America. To say that God has been good to me would be an understatement. I have had a truly wonderful life and I thank the Lord for it every day. But of all these different opportunities, homeschooling my children has been the greatest experience I have ever had.

My wife and I committed to one year at a time 15 years ago when the kids were little. We weren't sure we could handle it, and weren't sure exactly what we were doing, but we found amazing curriculum options and seasoned veterans willing to show us the ropes. And by the time we got seasoned ourselves at scheduling, memorizing, writing and reciting, we realized home schooling really wasn't about school. It was about time with our children. It was about creating a strong family, being their primary influence, cultivating lifelong relationships, and raising the next generation to stand with courage for the truth.

Yes, we love to see our children hard at work with pencil in hand. We love when they learn new things. We're free to direct their efforts to the things they excel in and free to go slow when they need extra help. And we are thrilled that they can help each other, because older children teaching their siblings bonds them and prepares them to home school their own children someday.

But it's our time with them that is the gift and the privilege. We have time to sort out opinions and direct them towards truth. We have time for lively discussions at unexpected moments. We have time to tackle the hard questions of life, and death and friendships. We have time to embark on great adventures together, to sing loud and long around the dinner table, and to practice fractions while baking for the neighbors. We have time to love each other and the many people, old and young, that God has put in our path to encourage and influence.

We are not spending this valuable time God has given us battling teachers and testing and peers and paperwork and obligatory make work projects. We are instead fine-tuning the character and morality of individuals, leaders and thinkers. We are learning as much when we clean the garage as when we study Antarctica and research how glass is made.

God has blessed me with wonderful opportunities but nothing compares to the quantity of quality time I spend with my children because of homeschooling. I love being with them. I love working with them. I love seeing them everyday. I love traveling with them. I cannot imagine someone else dictating to my children how, what and when to think. For us, homeschooling is a lifestyle. Learning happens everywhere. And sometimes it involves books.

My hope and prayer is that you will read this excellent book, and be influenced by it. I pray you will quickly begin what will likely become the greatest single adventure of your life. I know you can do it, and in the years to come, every sacrifice you make to home school will seem insignificant compared to the benefits of having wise children and a close, loving family.

Introduction

~

Hillary Clinton once defined education as "the most important non-family enterprise in the raising of the next generation." [1] Melissa Harris-Perry, an MSNBC show host, has opined, "So part of it is we have to break through our kind of private idea that kids belong to their parents or kids belong to their families, and recognize that kids belong to whole communities." [2]

Sam wrote this book to empower parents to reclaim their children from the State, to reject the assault on parenting that is so much a part of our society today. The two women quoted above, both mothers themselves, are collectivists in the worst possible sense of the term, and betray not only their gender, but also their brains. First, they are extraordinarily disrespectful toward women, implying that women are wholly inadequate at raising and educating their children. Second, by asserting that the child is not the parent's to nurture and instruct, as she or he knows best, they instead naively endow some governmental bureaucracy with encouraging, mothering characteristics, and parenting skills it cannot possibly possess. They are, in a word, ridiculous.

How did we get here? How did America get lulled into depositing our children in institutions each day, with strangers, believing they would 'turn out' just fine? I'm fine. You're fine. But youngsters today, are generally seemingly less-so. School shootings, ADD and other behavioral problems, drugs, sex – there are a lot of problems in the schools today, and it doesn't look like Hillary or Melissa, or really anyone in the establishment, is capable of fixing them.

Today, about 1.5 – 1.7 million American children are currently home-schooled. [3] Sam and I would like to see that number grow. It wasn't an obvious choice for us, though. Getting here was a journey that took some initiative, creativity, and a good amount of courage and dedication. So this book is intended to help make the transition to home education easier, simpler, and more relaxed than we had it! In short, our message is, "You can do this!"

When my wife Sam and I initially considered home schooling our three children, I was dead-set against it. First of all, my father was the junior high science teacher - public school was part of my heritage. Second, as a high school jock and all around popular guy, for me, school was a fantastic experience I'll never forget or regret. I still have good friends from my school days. No so, for my wife. Her school experience was somewhat traumatic, though not nearly as bad for her as other stories I've heard. She was bullied, and as a "brainiac," she was singled out by her schoolmates and picked on.

Our first son, Braeden, enjoyed school. He was a social kid who would talk to anyone. I used to take him with me to the grocery store, when he was 4 or 5, and he'd spontaneously start chatting with people in the produce aisle. "Hi," he'd begin. The unsuspecting shopper would look at the little kid riding in the cart, surprised into a response. "Hello, there!" they might answer.

Then Braeden would launch into a soliloquy of whatever popped into his creative little brain — and awkwardly, that often included me. "My name's Braeden. I'm four. My dad played Hercules on television. That's the strongest man in the world. Do you like bananas? I have a little brother named Shane. He farts, sometimes really bad, so the dog leaves the room. You know, that's a pretty bad fart!"

For Braeden's first grade, we moved into a new home and a new school district. We wanted suburban life, a big yard for the kids to play in. Frankly, I wanted to recreate my childhood. I had grown up on a dead end street in Minnesota with neighbor kids all around us. We would stay out playing until we heard our mothers standing on our back porches, yelling, "Dinner!" My parents came to every one of my basketball, football, or baseball games, and I was looking forward to reliving that period of my life vicariously through my kids.

When I would pick up Braeden from school in first grade, it

made me proud to witness the fruits of his outgoing personality. Though one of the youngest in the school, fifth graders knew his name. My boy had a winning way about him, but that kind of leadership manner can also lead to problems. I didn't really notice it at first, the change in my son, but once I did, it was unmistakable. My wife spent more time with him than I did, and she started talking to me about it. The fact was it was a very gradual shift of attitude, likely encouraged by the ageism that is inherent in the school system. It was almost thrust upon him, Braeden's *I'm-better-than-my-younger-siblings* worldview. The disharmony in our home was certainly our first clue, but it was subtle enough; we simply tried modifying and correcting his haughtiness. And that worked, too, though imperfectly.

There were other issues that came in later that Sam details in this book, which led us to make the shift to home education. I'll admit, like my wife, I was skeptical. Sam was up-close and personal with all the school stuff, and she convinced herself even before she came to me for my input. She insisted that I come on board, because we are a team, a unit, and she wouldn't have even tried if she couldn't convince me to join her. I listened to her rationale and took some time to digest it all. She reassured me that it was possibly a short-term proposition. It might not even be possible, but it was worth a try.

I'll admit there was a part of me that felt like I was letting down my dad. We were a family of 'team players.' Who was I to buck a system that had produced me? Not that I was the greatest thing since sliced bread, but I had turned out okay, hadn't I? And my school years were, in a word, awesome. Why deprive my kids of that amazing experience? What my wife was proposing was a kind of blasphemy. And yet...

There are no guarantees in life. The closest we come is the freedom we have in this country, and Lord knows even that's no longer a given. Sam was not convinced that our children were going to receive the education we wanted for them if we stayed in the public school — by all accounts one of the best schools around, and the one we moved house to attend!

She argued me down.

Kidding.

I considered her logic. It was unassailable. Reluctantly, I pondered trying it for just a semester, just to see. What might that look like? Then she hit me with the clincher. "Kevin, schools just aren't what they used to be. We have this romantic notion of what school is, but it's different today. There are drugs in schools today, and the more affluent the school, sometimes the worse the drug problem. No one is safe. The system that you and I grew up under is broken, and I don't think we should be trusting it."

So it really all boiled down to trust. Sam had articulated exactly what I had been feeling but unable to realistically identify until that moment, because my sight was clouded by my own experiences, great ones, of growing up in a small town in another century – That was then, and this is now. Now, we live in a world of cell phones, Internet, electronic gaming, bullying and rampant drug use. Let's face it; the world has changed substantially. Above all, it was a time when our schools delivered as a matter of principle. Now, not only don't they deliver, but even that principle is in question. Plus, they demand more and more money, for what they themselves admit is inferior results.

Maybe you are like me, hoping against hope that it will all simply work out for them, like it did for us. We weathered the storms in our school years, so our kids will, too. But if you, like me, have that small seed of doubt, if you sense there is something intrinsically wrong with sending your child to *that* school, and if you suspect there might be better choices available to you, well, I'm here to encourage you to explore you options.

Ultimately, Sam and I made a choice for family over tradition. A tradition is only worthwhile if it is beneficial. We discovered, as you will read in these pages, that the tradition of public school is actually harmful, in too many cases. We took the bold step to bring our kids home, and we've never regretted it. I hope you do the same. If you have kids and are wondering about the home school option, I hope this book blesses you and your family. They are **YOUR** kids, after all.

~ Kevin Sorbo

WHY HOME SCHOOL?

~

The Reluctant Radical

~

"There is exactly one authentically radical social movement of any real significance in the United States, and it is not Occupy, the Tea Party, or the Ron Paul faction. It is homeschoolers, who, by the simple act of instructing their children at home, pose an intellectual, moral, and political challenge to the government-monopoly schools, which are one of our most fundamental institutions and one of our most dysfunctional. Like all radical movements, homeschoolers drive the establishment bats." [4]

I was modeling in the Seychelles Islands, on assignment for the well-known French magazine, *Madame Figaro*. The islands were overgrown and under-populated, leaving acres of sparkling white sand beaches, groves of swaying palms, and the clear aqua water lapping at the shoreline virtually untouched and certainly private. The sun was hot but not oppressive; the breeze floating by tickled the back of my neck.

It was a ten-day trip, and it had taken a long, aggravating time to get there from Paris, because the Seychelles Islands are off the east coast of Africa. We stayed in the only hotel on our island. It was a cozy type of place, composed of a main lodge, built of sizable log-poles and a thatched roof. It was primitive, but functional. The rooms, comprised of individual small thatch-roofed bungalows, perched a distance from the lodge. At night there was no sound but leaves rattling and animals announcing themselves.

These modeling trips were always unique, and I never knew precisely what to expect. In fact, I've taken assignments with the same photographer and catalog envisioning déjà vu, only to be disappointed by a completely different dynamic. If there was one person who could dictate the tone of the trip, it would be the client, who, for the purposes of my story here, was the editor. She ran the show. The client, or editor, foots the bill. Everyone must ingratiate themselves to the one with the money and power. A trip might be great, with everyone getting along, or horrible, with infighting and uncomfortable situations. Of course, my overall enjoyment also largely depended on my fellow models, who could be petty, aggressive, or a whole lot of fun, and I had experienced a vast array.

Our stylist, a thin, controlling woman in her sixties, was a fashion savant - she lived and breathed clothes and had been at the magazine for at least a lifetime, which is saying something in this quixotic and fickle industry. She suffered tremendous migraines, and had been experiencing a particularly grievous one since arriving, or maybe before. She set a tense undertone for the entire trip. I remember the make-up artist telling me how anxious she was. As proof, she placed my hand on her belly, which was rock-solid, though not flat. "I haven't gone to the toilet for a week. It's all just in there, and it's not coming out. Hard as a *rock!*"

I found it odd that she would share such an intimate and embarrassing detail with me. Maybe she needed to explain why she wouldn't wear a bathing suit on the beach, where we shot photos most days. On a shoot, in a foreign land, members of the group can become intimate friends — but only for the time you are there together. It is seldom those friendships endure, and this trip would be no different in that regard. But it did change my life dramatically.

"Done drink de punch." The Parisian hairdresser spoke slowly and leaned close to my ear. He had a French accent, and although it irked me a tiny bit that he chose to speak to me in English, I was too intrigued to be bothered.

I tilted my head to look at him and whispered back, "Why not?"

He grinned with mischief. "We're trying to get the stylist high. I'm only letting you know because I can tell you don't do drugs. Ne le bois pas!"

I said, "Okay," and thought, "Wow. Is it that obvious I'm a goody two-shoes?"

The subject of drugs had not yet come up in our group, to my knowledge. Thinking back, I suppose if the other model and photographer were off getting high each night, I wouldn't know. They were dating. For that matter, the entire crew could be doing things at night that I wasn't privy to. I liked to read after dinner, not being much of a social butterfly, although I would always go to a meal with the group if that's what they were doing, especially on an island that provided no other distractions. A girl's gotta eat.

I'd never been a radical, used alcohol or drugs, or suffered through any traditional teenage rebellion phase. My follow-the-rules behavior stuck out in the midst of the hedonistic, impetuous fashion community. And for some reason, the hair-dresser decided to protect me from what he somehow knew I would consider a horrible violation, though he certainly didn't see it as such. To him, the stylist was the target.

Today, I feel a little like the hair-dresser in my story. I'm trying to warn people not to drink the punch that the public, and some private, schools have spiked with a drug far more dangerous than a chemical one that wears off after a few hours. The drug they are using is a lifelong enslavement into poverty of thought. Convincing parents that they are ill equipped for the task of teaching their own children, the public school system has become a placebo for true learning, hollow, fake, and centered on a political agenda. This in no way reflects on the intention of many educators who came to the system for the right reasons but lack the system's support to succeed in the ways they planned. I will explain...

An Innocent Beginning...

My home school journey had an innocent beginning. My actor husband travels a good deal for work. His television series had ended, and films don't shoot in the same location all the time. Understanding that frequent or prolonged separation is difficult on a couple and a family, we made a commitment to never be apart for longer than two weeks. If Kevin was to shoot a movie in New

Orleans for two months, I traveled out with the children for the middle portion of it, or he came back home in-between.

I was accustomed to travel from my career as a model, and if that was the way for me to spend time with my husband (and keep my marriage) then so be it.

I should also mention here that we moved into a great new community at the time my oldest child began first-grade, nearly to the day. We chose our new home for the well-rated public schools. My children were enrolled in this understanding public school that was willing to accommodate our frequent family travel, for only two years. During Biwa's second grade, I faced a challenge I had never imagined.

Biwa, my oldest, and I sat in Kevin's trailer, on set in Hawaii while he was shooting "Soul Surfer," trying to finish an assignment so that when Kevin was released for his precious half-hour break for lunch, we would be available. Biwa and I hovered over his strangely confusing second-grade worksheets, trying to figure out what the teacher wanted him to do on this particular assignment. Frustrated and anxious to be finished, Biwa said to me, "Mom, my teacher told me I didn't even have to do these!"

"Well, Biwa, she gave them to me with the specific instructions that you were supposed to do them, so I highly doubt…"

"But Mom, in class, she says they aren't necessary, because there isn't enough time."

It dawned on me right then: This busy-work had to be turned in, so she could report he had done *something* - *anything* - to ensure the school could collect their money for Biwa's attendance. That's how it works in school. *Check the box.*

Then I had my second epiphany. *I* was the *substitute* teacher! And it didn't feel so good; frankly, arguing with my child over what the teacher wanted him to do, versus what Mommy required. Why was I suddenly pitted against the teacher in this scenario? I didn't fit in this role. This was my child, made from Kevin's and my DNA. No one knew him better than we did and I knew that grade school material well enough to teach it to him backwards.

I dug a blank notepad out of Biwa's backpack. We started back at the top, reviewing the principles of addition. I made some practice problems for him to do. Our disconnect dissolved instantly, Biwa looking to me for knowledge, reaffirming his and my faith in me as a mentor and parent. Because I'm a team player and, in my mind, still part of the education conglomerate, I had Biwa finish what he could of the silly worksheets - the ones none of the other kids were doing. But I also began to consider home schooling as the solution to my problems.

The final epiphany is this set of three would come later, when I realized the school structure of sending work home is strangely geared to form a wedge between the parent and the child. Too nefarious of a concept for me to digest then, it would dawn on me slowly. I don't mean to intimate this is a purposeful set-up, but I do contend that sending homework home with children who have been in schools for a full day already, is not a recipe for a successful home life.

I loved being with my kids, and I was thrilled to see them learn and grow. The more I considered keeping them home, the more I resented the loss of sending them away to someone else for instruction.

The full transition for me happened over the summer, after school was finished, and while I 'tried on' the home school mantle. I bought the kids workbooks to do over the summer, something I did every year, anyway, but I started taking it a bit more seriously. Planning ahead, I researched curricula, read up on reviews, and studied education books. As I researched how to educate my children, I unexpectedly learned how our public education system fails, and, to a large extent, how to combat it. I don't have all the answers—especially not for our schools. I do know now that when parents wave goodbye at the schoolhouse gate, it's not just to their kids, but often, in part, to their relationships. Additionally, teachers can't instill the requisite knowledge during the time allotted — they've admitted as much by the quantity of homework they send home at the end of each day. That's only the beginning of where our schools fail to live up to their mandate.

Have You Heard of Common Core?

Common Core is the name of the new standard, and although proponents insist it is not a curriculum, it imposes conformity on curricula while promising improved learning and more *standardized* materials. This is why so many textbooks are now labeled "Common Core Aligned." Common Core has been debunked by many established education professionals like Professor of Education Reform Sandra Stotsky and Senior Policy Advisor for the Office of Planning, Evaluation and Policy Development at the U.S. Department of Education Ze'ev Wurman, among countless others. They contend that, among other things, Common Core seems to simply level the field of *achievement.* That's what *standardized* stands for. By striving for uniformity, it establishes and systematizes contempt for exceptionalism, and reverence for mediocrity. For instance, it delays teaching eighth-grade algebra until ninth grade (holding back the advanced to allow other to 'catch up'), and substitutes technical manuals for English literature. That's sold to parents as an improvement of standards.

Common Core conspicuously fails to address the disconnection between parents' reasonable expectations and the school's limitations, the gap into which many children stumble and fall. Our schools don't lack materials so much as methodology. When observant (and financially able) parents discover this, they often also realize they have few choices but private or home school.

I chose to home school my children, and I am grateful for the choice I made.

Home schooling families are generally counter-culture and anti-establishment. However, we have one strong distinction from other radical groups — most home schoolers don't demand educational system revision. We don't impose our views on others, but only seek freedom to pursue our options. We may encourage and advocate for home schooling, but this originates from the near-universal desire for the improvement of education on behalf of all children. We also recognize that fringe positions don't change entrenched systems overnight.

The one danger home educators pose to the establishment is success. Their education strategies, with their exceptional results, have attracted attention, which serves to highlight the problems of the educational establishment, including Common Core. While comprising only 2% of the general school-aged population, home schooled children make up ten percent of spelling bee finalists,.

"The recent successes of home schoolers in these contests have been very beneficial for home education, because it now becomes credible to many people who were thinking before that this is just done by a bunch of weirdos who want to go in the back woods and isolate their children," says Michael Smith, the president of the Home School Legal Defense Association.[5]

Typically, home educators don't pursue controversy, but have experienced it as the establishment has distanced itself from them, most recently by implementing Common Core. The home schooling parent most often seeks to elevate their children, while the education system institutes a plan that lowers expectations of achievement, and abandons the goal of challenging each student to learn, explore, and excel as they best can, individually. Many of the parents choose to shield their children from the education conglomerate because they admire *uniqueness,* but they have concluded that the current bureaucracy promotes *homogeneity.*

School bureaucrats view homogeneity as a desirable outcome, as if education could mimic a fast-food franchise. Think of the unspoken slogans: "Blend in," "Don't attract attention," and "Don't stick your neck out." This must confuse children. On the one hand, schools teach "fairness" and "equality of outcomes," while, on the other, society publicly and loudly lifts up those who excel. Witness the media attention we give to TV, movie, and reality "stars," as well as politicians and business leaders, who excel. True, often their talents entangle them in great failures and scandals, but lauded they continue to be, anyway. How is that *fair* and *equal*?

Average Versus Exceptional

Our current educational system seems to honor average rather than exceptional performance, refusing to encourage students to develop the skills and qualities of leadership. More importantly, our schools no longer produce students who can compete internationally. According to Pearson, a multinational education company, the US ranks fourteenth of forty developed nations tested for 'cognitive skills and educational attainment.' We rank twenty-fourth in literacy.[6]

How to correct the downward achievement spiral? The establishment implements Common Core, an untested new strategy, amidst great secrecy and controversy. Parents rightly doubt the ability of the educational establishment to heal itself.

Many of them have turned towards the home school option, calculating that they can do as well or better than the mediocre results of our current education system. A person who acts in opposition to the accepted standard is considered a radical. I know. I am one, now.

I encourage parents who desire exceptional achievement for their children to accept the dare indirectly thrust on us by our education bureaucracy. Home educate your children, and if that's not an option, certainly consider a private Christian school for them. This book is for every parent, especially those who say, "I couldn't possibly do that. I don't have that kind of relationship with my child." (By the way, "anymore" is implied in that sentence.)

Case in point:

Recently I talked to a frustrated young mom. Not only had her son been unchallenged at school, he kept asking why he was forced to do busy work when he'd already learned the material. His ongoing misery made her rethink her belief that she *couldn't* do it. She just needed to figure out *how* to get it done.

As a writer who needed peace and quiet to work, she reasonably feared she would forfeit her own important solitude. Things got too difficult, though, and she felt home school was the only way forward. They stepped off the cliff, and were astonished at the incredible blessing it turned out to be. After a brief period of acclimation, they both discovered they loved the new paradigm. To her delight, she soon discovered home education increased freedom for both of them, because home schooling doesn't demand one-on-one interaction eight hours a day, but it does release the parent from the institution's schedule and other demands of traditional school. Her son's transformed attitude energized him to complete his schoolwork in record time each day, which enabled him to pursue other interests.

Another bonus became their reestablished relationship once he was out of the stifling school environment. During the years that he attended the public school, there had been a gradual deterioration of their communication and mutual affection. With certain corrupting influences removed (no more fighting over homework, for instance), not only did they recapture a solid relationship, but his interactions with his younger sister improved, as well.

Many of us don't feel capable of taking on the education of our children, ourselves. This, of course, is a self-defeating attitude fostered by the establishment. But let me address, for a moment, the story of a single dad who was convinced he couldn't home school because he had to work. When it became evident that his son was not thriving in school, Dad decided to try a different approach. He worked out an arrangement with his manager to allow him to work partially from home, and hired a tutor to home school the boy during the time he would be away. Sometimes, he brought his boy with him to meetings, to sit quietly, reading, while he conducted his business. No one would have thought this arrangement possible, before he tried it. Where there's a will, there's a way.

There is also the now famous story of Dr. Ben Carson's mother, who did her own version of home education, by insisting her children turn in book reports to her, in addition to attending school — reports she herself couldn't read. Simply her devotion and insistence impressed upon young Ben the importance of an education, the repercussions of which we can see today in his incredible medical successes and his bid for the presidency of this nation.

Your family can also benefit from home education. If you are reading this book, you are already thinking about alternatives to traditional schooling. This book is designed to help you make an informed decision about whether you should home school. (You should.)

I begin with an honest assessment on the state of our schools. It saddens me no end to see how far our education system has sunk. If you are already familiar with the problem, feel free to skip right to the solution! The second part of the book is devoted to giving the reader a glimpse into the life of a home school family. We are not the *perfect* home school family, but we are representative! I know if I had had the chance to see behind the curtain before I started out home schooling, it might have made my journey a little less stressful.

The best way to avoid the issues of our deteriorating schools and teachers' unions — and their bastard child, Common Core — is with the most obvious alternative, the Common Sense choice: home schooling.

Believe me, it isn't what you think. And it's so much better than you could possibly hope!

THE STATE OF OUR SCHOOLS

~

"Nothing in all the world is more dangerous than sincere ignorance and conscientious stupidity."
~ Martin Luther King Jr., *Strength to Love,* 1963

It's the first day of preschool for my first-born. He's so excited to go, but also a bit apprehensive. I'm excited for him, too, because this is the start for him to make friends and discover the world outside. Home schooling isn't even on my radar, and I wouldn't have considered preschool, but my girlfriend, Braeden's best friend's mom, introduced me to a wonderful little Montessori preschool in Canada, where we live. It's close to the house, half day, and the director is fantastic - I can sense that she really understands education as a way to engage the natural curiosity of children.

The first day arrives and Braeden and I saddle up. He wants to do everything himself: put on his shoes, open the door, climb into his car seat, and buckle it himself. But he's too slow. If he doesn't hurry, we'll be late, and that's not acceptable. The teacher has agreed to meet me at the door, so I don't have to unload my infant, Shane, in order to walk Braeden into the classroom. I'm stressed. "Hurry up, Braeden! We've got to go! You don't want to be late, do you?"

Understand that "late" to a toddler is meaningless. I might as well be talking to myself.

We drive to the school and, as promised, Mina greets us at the doorway. Braeden suddenly turns shy. Mina deftly says, "Did you think I wouldn't be here to greet you? Of course I am! Come along, now..." and she whisks him away from me.

That was hard. Tears in my eyes, I get back in the car with the baby. It turned out Braeden only cried a few times the first days of going to that school. He loved his time there, with Mina. But after we moved, I enrolled him in another "Montessori" preschool. This second one only offered full days, and Braeden cried every single time I dropped him off. To this day I carry the guilt of abandoning him there. It was entirely unnecessary. Once my younger children were ready for preschool, I also enrolled them in what I thought was a lovely little school that sat at the top of a hillside, with lots of outdoor areas and things to do in the classroom. They lasted about two weeks, before I pulled them both out. There was a young girl in one of the classes - and all the classes were close to each other, who cried incessantly. Every time I was there, she was crying, sometimes softly, sometimes wailing, sometimes being comforted, but most often being ignored by the teachers. How could I leave my children there when they clearly did not wish it? Now, I am more convinced than ever that preschool is a waste of time. Play school can be fun, sure, but only if the child really wants it.

Suzie is excited for her first day of first grade, but also a little scared. Mom and Dad approach the day with both pride and trepidation. It is an exhilarating milestone, certainly, but they also feel like they are jumping off a cliff. What if Suzie doesn't like her teacher? What if Suzie has trouble making friends? School, as they remember it, is fraught with pitfalls and dangers, as well as opportunities to triumph. They are apprehensive of the unknown. Mom and Dad are there to hand precious little Suzie off to a complete stranger, the teacher that school administrators have randomly chosen from the options they have, teachers who are protected by their unions, not necessarily retained because of good past performance.

Think of this for a moment. We teach our children never to talk to strangers. We surreptitiously screen other parents before we allow play dates for our kids. (Do you allow your kids to drink soda? Play video games all day? Have lots of candy?) And yet, when it comes to school, we pass our children off to a complete stranger, chosen, often at random, by other strangers who have elevated them to this level of responsibility, within a bureaucracy that is self-admittedly flawed.

Mom and Dad have faith in the school *institution*, probably because this is the way it's always been (from what they remember, anyway) and because nearly everybody else does it this way. *If everyone was jumping off the bridge, would you jump, too?*

So, sweet, innocent little Suzie takes a seat in first grade with Miss Maple, who seems really nice, during the few moments Mom and Dad met with her in the chaos that comprises the first morning at school. Suzie cried a little, but Mom promised to be there at the end of the day, and, well, she *has* to go to school, right? Never mind the tears; this is how it's done: Suzie's first lesson in conformity.

At lunch, Suzie pulls out her special packed lunch that Mom and Dad worked together to make her. Dad put some chips for her into a plastic zip-lock baggie, and Mom carefully placed some chocolate pieces right on top of her sandwich. Suzie smiles, feeling special. But Miss Maple doesn't like plastic bags. She tells the class, holding up Suzie's lunch as an example, that plastic bags are bad for the landfills. They don't disintegrate, and they get swept out into the ocean, which can hurt the wildlife! Miss Maple also writes a quick note while she explains to Suzie that candy is not allowed, unless there is enough for the whole class. Miss Maple only deals in environmentalism and equality, and while she uses Suzie as an example for the whole class, she makes it clear the problem isn't little Suzie; it's her mom and dad. Lesson number two: parents are wrong and the teacher is the ultimate arbiter of good and evil. These lessons will continue, subtly and otherwise, every day that Suzie attends school. Can we blame Suzie for rebelling as a teenager?

Trouble Born In the Classroom

"I could never home-school. I'd probably kill my kid by Wednesday, if I had to spend the entire day with him, every day." I have heard this countless times, most recently from a third-grade public school teacher, about her own kids (not the ones she teaches, of course...)! I couldn't help but wonder that other parents would blindly trust her with their children. They are simply relying on the integrity of the institution.

Sadly, this generally combative attitude represents typical rhetoric for many teen-parent relationships. Ironically, the parents who say these kind of things are often ideal candidates for home schooling. But ask them how their parent-child relationship deteriorated to this point, and they would be hard-pressed to give you an answer. The short version is, it's not their fault.

Possibly the worst thing frustrated parents do is send their aloof, argumentative children to public school. In a sense, dropping them somewhere, for others to deal with, might be considered *giving up on the relationship*. Children aren't stupid. They may reasonably perceive the decision to let the school cope with them as a form of rejection. Some might suggest that school offers parents a socially acceptable way to avoid resolving challenges with their kids, as they turn them over to professional educators. While that's cynical, the truth is actually worse. The public education system *encourages* parents to disengage from their children. This is why it isn't the parents' fault.

If parents can't spend time with their children, how will they communicate love to them? Many parents are so blinded by the school's promise of education as the way to prepare kids for success in life that they cannot see the issues (educational or social) that might be cause for concern. They hustle their kids into the wolves' den and wonder why their children return home behaving like wild animals.

What Children Learn in School

Parents who puzzle over their distant relationship with their teen often miss the obvious answer. They relinquished the majority of their influence the moment their children crossed public school's threshold, way back in kindergarten or first grade. It's that simple. Each day, children are subtly encouraged to view their parents as ignorant adults who don't know everything — eventually, perhaps, even as people who don't know anything. Kids reinforce this by repeating instructions from their acknowledged authority, the teachers. They don't hesitate to scold their parents, as they are taught to do: "Don't put plastic sandwich bags in my lunch. You're killing the dolphins."

In their minds, the teacher cares about wildlife, but Daddy kills innocent marine animals. Children learn to challenge authority (and please consider that parents are *moral* authority), and then those same youngsters assert themselves at home, voicing the criticisms learned at school.

Often parents rationalize a child's attitude — "Well, that's probably a good thing, because they're learning to be self-confident and capable," — even while they suspect that something isn't quite right.

Troubled Teens

A few years later, these surly, judgmental offspring — now teenagers — instigate fights too big for parents to try to win anymore. In the resulting impasse, parents throw up their hands in frustration. "Teenagers!" Many of their friends face the same situation of the seemingly inevitable negative transformation. These teens with inflated egos insist on independence, expressing disdain for Mom's and Dad's outdated values, and resenting their parents' control of the television remote or access to the car or finances.

Rather than help resolve these fractured relationships and reinforce parental authority, the public school 'experts' soothe parental concerns saying, "We see this kind of thing every day. You just need to stay calm and weather the storm."

Other parents agree. They accept the view that the teenaged years will be the pits, with challenges to authority, emotional distancing, and unreasonable argumentativeness. In so doing they "drink the punch" about dysfunction and shrug it off as completely normal and acceptable.

By "normal" they mean that *most* children go through this, but *most* children are enrolled in public school.

Acquaintances of mine went to a home schooling convention when their children were young and met families with polite, loving teenagers. They quickly decided, "That's how we want our kids to behave when they're that age." Now they successfully home school their respectful and caring teens.

Obviously, the image I am painting may be somewhat extreme. Not all home-schooled children are angels as teenagers, and not every youth in public school is an angry rebel. My illustrations should serve to show the mechanisms behind some common family dynamics and how they might be improved. Someone said to me the other day, "All teens rebel." I laughed, because I distinctly remember *not* rebelling at all, despite a public school education and an absentee single parent. I'll concede that parents and children are all unique individuals, if my critics will acknowledge that risks abound. As parents, we must learn to play the odds. With home schooling and the enduring relationships it fosters, I like my chances much better.

Excuses, excuses...

Excuses *not* to home-school abound.

"I'm too busy. It's all I can do to keep up with their homework."

"I can't teach my kids. What would I do when they got to algebra or calculus? I don't remember *any* of that stuff."

"Home school *my* kid? Too much work!"

"Are you kidding? Somebody's gotta work for a living!"

"Educate them myself? Isn't that why I pay my taxes?"

These distressing declarations forewarn of a tremendous loss: the deterioration of their parent-child relationships. Tragically, these parents have naïvely placed their hope and trust in an institutionalized public education bureaucracy that has declined dramatically over the years. Rather than push their kids to learn, respect others, and excel in order to make a positive difference, it encourages kids to do the opposite. Today's education gradually and thoroughly destroys the enthusiasm of the child and the fabric of family life and, consequently, the future roles of both in our nation.

If you believe that first grade learning is too hard to attempt, send your children to public school. But let's not fool ourselves:

homework *is* home school, just with more pressure, later in the day, when everyone's tired, hungry, and grouchy.

Challenges in the System

In his book, *The Underground History of American Education,* John Taylor Gatto comments on age-graded schools:

> *"The socialization of children in age-graded groups monitored by State agents is essential to learn to get along with others in a pluralistic society. The actual truth is that the rigid compartmentalizations of schooling teach a crippling form of social relation: wait passively until you are told what to do, never judge your own work or confer with associates, have contempt for those younger than yourself and fear of those older. Behave according to the meaning assigned to your class label. These are the rules of a nuthouse."*[7]

What other place in society divides people by their age, down to the year? Even the medical community brackets people in multiple-year age groups to process patient information. While children have similar development *patterns*, these vary wildly in *timing*. It would seem more logical, in an academic environment, to place them according to their scholastic abilities. Yet public schools divide them by a single factor, the only value of which is expedience.

In *Age-Grading is a Bad Idea*, Gary North expounds on the reasons why we age-grade, none of which have anything to do with serving our kids.

> *"The system rested on grade-specific textbooks which had to provide continuity from grade to grade. The teachers could no longer do this. They did not know what was taught to students above or below their age-specific grades. This removed the teacher from the overall educational program. The teacher became an isolated cog in a bureaucratic machine. It placed administrators in charge. They designed*

the curriculum. They chose the textbooks. They ran the experiments. They adopted the fads, which came and went."[8]

Originally, age grading was a cost-cutting tool. It later became apparent that separating children by age, and isolating teachers to specific sub-groups of children, was even more useful to the upper echelons of the school staff. Administrators compartmentalized the various grades and subjects, making teachers interchangeable (read expendable), organizing the system to further solidify their power. They seem selfishly motivated, without consideration for the children who would fall outside of the rigid lines they drew for the masses. As is often the case, the administrators looked for the best way to maintain the organization and their job security, with minimal focus on the outcome for the children, while plausibly exclaiming "expediency!"

Consider that we systemically fail to honor our elderly, offering the older generation less respect than ever before. Families no longer take care of parents at home, but instead, stash them in a variety of facilities. As a result, the assisted living market is thriving and families are experiencing additional disconnect with older members.

Instilling ageism through our schools for a century has played a part in dismantling the relationships between all generations, not just parent-child. If unspoken resentment or fear of older people is fostered in children, it's unreasonable to expect them to grow into individuals who honor their elders, including their parents. Repercussions of this form of ageism permeate our society. Because it's far enough removed from the sources of this distancing, most people miss the connection.

The antiquated one-room schoolhouse system, without age-specific separation, was far more effective than our current model at instilling the values, knowledge, and abilities we prized then and those we should value today. Many members of the Greatest Generation, our national heroes, came from one-room schools. Are we now content to call ourselves the "Not-So-Bad Generation?

THE HOMEWORK EPIPHANY

~

"The unions are the worst thing that ever happened to education because it's not a meritocracy. It turns into a bureaucracy, which is exactly what has happened. The teachers can't teach and administrators run the place and nobody can be fired. It's terrible."

~ Steve Jobs[9]

In 2009 my first-born attended second grade in our local public school. Although he spent over six hours a day there, he had tons of homework. I wondered, "Why am I sending my kids to school, when the school sends them back to me to educate?"

A friend complained to me that when her son had to do a book report, she had to spend at least five hours of her own time working on it with him. Another parent told me how great the tutoring was at the franchise down the street from her. All this made me ask, if I'm ultimately in charge of my kids' education, why do I feel so powerless?

Some Fundamentals

I approached education with the belief that the government knew best what, and how, to teach my kids. It was an assumption I was raised with and had never before challenged. Well, you know what they say about you when you assume...

The economic collapse several years ago dragged me, kicking and screaming, to question the efficacy and intelligence of our representatives in Washington. I place the blame squarely on the shoulders of our representatives in Washington who try, however ill advisedly, to regulate what ought to be a free market. Frankly, things since then have done nothing to renew my confidence, and that's an understatement. Since the housing calamity, we now have the lowest percentage of home ownership since the 1960's; all because Jimmy Carter, Bill Clinton, Barney Frank, and Fanny Mae *intended* to make housing more affordable.

Thanks to their good intentions, coupled with the Washington spenders, the economy is in the tank; we don't have a balanced budget, and don't get me started on the deficit. Most of us agree that something is seriously wrong. When the government can't balance its own checkbook and simply prints more money—that becomes a problem for all of us.

My long-standing assumptions about education crumbled under new scrutiny. Is our failing government the best resource for guidance? Should our tax dollars be funneled through an inefficient bureaucracy, sifted by the teaching lobby, one of the most powerful lobbies ever in Washington, and, finally, returned, filtered down and diluted, to our children? Then again, why is education an entitlement provided by the US government? Why are we tolerating the scam that there is no more money for our schools (or the swindle that money will fix them,) while elected officials continue to send money overseas to fund things like "Worldwide Cultural Preservation"[10] — to the tune of more than $20 million since 2001? I realized it was time for me to do some homework.

Academics?

On December 6th, 2010, President Obama addressed a report that US teens continue to sink in world education rankings, calling for another "Sputnik moment." It took eighteen years to bring our space program up to par when we were running second in the race. According to the *Programme for International Student Assessment* (PISA)[11], in a recent study of sixty-five countries, US education scored lower than fourteenth in three different categories on the list, well behind Japan and South Korea.

Weigh the costs of a mediocre public education. It puts your parent-child relationship at risk. It diminishes the child's opportunity to learn to excel. It overemphasizes socialization while sending home work that could have (should have) been done in class.

On the other hand, home-schooled children typically out-perform their public school counterparts by 30-37 percentile points across the board, because their academic time is better structured. They have better relationships with family members, in part due to socializing and sharing interests with children of different ages.

Common Sense points to the advantages of home education in nurturing and instruction. Despite our social conditioning that predisposes us favorably toward public education, responsible parents owe it to themselves and to their families to investigate this alternate option.

Follow the Money

In California, the biggest teachers union spent $212 million over the past decade in political lobbying, money that at one point was tax dollars. These funds flowed from We the People through a paper-maché bureaucracy, sometimes directly past the teachers, and into the union coffers. The teachers' unions negotiate with the government they help to elect, hardly an arms-length transaction.

> *Between 1990 and 2010, 93 percent of donations made by National Education Association political action committees and individual officers went to Democrats, according to OpenSecrets.org. According to the NEA's own "Status of the American Public School Teacher 2005-2006,"* [12] *(latest available data produced March 2010) only 41 percent of public school teachers are Democrats. A Wall Street Journal editorial revealed that the National Education Association — the nation's largest teachers union — "is spending the mandatory dues paid by members who are told their money will be used to gain better wages, benefits and working conditions. According to the latest filing, member dues accounted for $295 million of the NEA's $341 million in total receipts last year. But the union spent $25 million of that on 'political activities and lobbying' and another $65.5*

million on 'contributions, gifts and grants' that seemed designed to further those hyper-liberal political goals." [13]

Teachers' unions aren't the only problem. Minnesota schools start *after* Labor Day because the Tourism and State Fair lobbyists insist the State Fair is a crucial weekend for tourism and local dollars. This seems to imply that the State Fair takes precedence over education. At least, the money it generates does.

Money runs the show, and that's why many are convinced it can fix the system. They're not only wrong; they're one hundred and eighty degrees wrong and thus, are part of the problem, though some of them don't even know it. Misuse of money has broken the system, but human greed is *why* it's broken and greed can't be repaired. Greed is part of human nature. It is a spiritual problem that seemingly no one in the public is willing to fight head-on. So the unions and the government clamor for more money, and the fawning sycophants line their own pockets. Spiritual problems cannot be solved with physical solutions. More money has never solved the problems of the wayward education bureaucracies, and it never will. The education establishment must return to being more about the advancement of education in our children, and less about power and money. And the only way to do that is to wrest the power away from the institution, bringing the educational responsibility back home.

Paid Not *to Teach*

Teachers' unions protect teachers' jobs, to the detriment of learning, by funneling money to non-working teachers. A teacher can be removed from the classroom as a result of, for example, alleged misconduct or failure to follow the curriculum. That teacher then receives *full pay* while awaiting the administrative review process, which takes somewhere between a long time and forever. In 2012 alone idle teachers reportedly cost New York State $30 million, because union laws prevented their dismissal.

That's a lot of computer labs and art classes. One teacher, who allegedly told a student she had a "sexy body", continued to collect his $100,000 salary while he ran a law practice and real estate business, because they couldn't fire him.[14]

In 2009, LAUSD was paying full salaries to some 160 teachers who were waiting for accusations of misconduct to be resolved. Those were the teachers who were *not* teaching, and we foolishly complain about the ones who *are*. To add insult to insufferable injury, our schools' budgets are being cut. Perhaps there's just not enough money to pay all the teachers for *not* teaching our kids.

The good news (for some) is that President Obama signed a $26 billion bill to save teaching, and other public servant jobs. That ought to make the lobbyists really happy.

Arne Duncan, the American Education Secretary, commented on The PISA, which collects test results from 65 countries, and more than half a million students, to rank them in education standings every three years. He called the PISA findings a "picture of educational stagnation." He told the Associated Press that America needs to "invest in early education, raise academic standards, make college affordable, and do more to recruit and retain top-notch educators."[15]

Please note that his first critique is concerned with funds. More money, *more money*! According to the PISA assessment, "While the U.S. spends more per student than most countries, this does not translate into better performance. For example, the Slovak Republic, which spends around $53,000 per student, performs at the same level as the United States, which spends over $115,000 per student."[16] That's more than twice as much, for equal results.

Choosing Sides

Evidence points to illogical and inefficient government solutions, but the government insists it has the answer. That's what I call job-security. In the interest of sustaining an ever-increasing bureaucracy, our government continues to present itself as the only entity capable of addressing all the challenges of life.

"Give me your money, and I will take care of everything," is the government's unspoken motto. As a result of misplaced trust in the government by the majority of Americans, we believe and want to continue to trust that our government *will* take care of things. Perhaps this is because of the illusion of safety in numbers, or maybe it's simply a desire to avoid personal liability. After all, it's easier when you can blame someone else for mistakes. But reason presses us to question how well that's really working out for We the People.

It isn't. Our public schools are failing. Dropouts occur earlier than ever before, not simply in high school, but in middle school, as well. California has a dropout rate exceeding 11%, with some students dropping out as early as fifth grade. About four out of five students who entered high school in fall 2010 graduated last June, or 80.8 percent. But 11.6 percent of those destined for the class of 2014 dropped out before even entering high school, up from 11.4 percent for the previous year's class.[17] While this statistic might be good enough to recommend a chewing gum, is it enough to recommend investing more tax dollars?

Every year, over 1.2 million students drop out of high school in the United States alone. That's a student every 26 seconds – or 7,000 a day. About 25% of high school freshmen fail to graduate from high school on time. The U.S., which had some of the highest graduation rates of any developed country, now ranks 22nd out of 27 developed countries.[18] The trend indicates failure, not success.

My friend's kid goes to one of the top-rated public schools. "Top-rated," compared to what? The best of the worst is still one of the worst.

HUMAN RIGHTS

~

"A thorough knowledge of the Bible is worth more than a college education."
~ Theodore Roosevelt[19]

What Sets US Apart...

The Department of Education's mission statement reads:

Our mission is to promote student achievement and preparation for global competitiveness by fostering educational excellence and ensuring equal access.

Ask yourself how they are going to do that, given the constraints of federal law, as it is written (below).

Federal law prohibits the federal government from dictating educational curriculum content to the nation's public schools. In fact, according to independent legal research conducted by the Pioneer Institute, no less than three separate statutes prohibit this from happening.

Yet on President Barack Obama's watch, there has been a concerted effort within his administration to control public education with the Common Core agenda. Back in 2009 and 2010 when the administration was distributing so-called "stimulus" funds, the U.S. Department of Education devised what was called the "Race to the Top" initiative. Public schools could apply for and receive the stimulus money, but they had to meet specific criteria.[20]

Our education system, which was established with the cabinet level Department of Education agency in 1980 during the Carter administration, offers an example of the inefficacy of government institutions. Revamped every few years with new initiatives to 'benefit' our kids, its stated mission "is to promote student achievement and preparation for global competitiveness by fostering educational excellence and ensuring equal access."

Where the Money Goes

With 4,400 employees and a *$68 billion budget*, you'd expect a top-notch education system, but our students score only "*average*" in math and science when compared to other developed nations. So how is the money being spent? The following shows the intention of the U. S. Department of Education for allocating their funds.

- Establishing policies on federal financial aid for education, and distributing as well as monitoring those funds.
- Collecting data on America's schools and disseminating research.
- Focusing national attention on key educational issues.
- Prohibiting discrimination and ensuring equal access to education.
-

None of these goals focus on improving academics. Billions of dollars do *nothing* to develop academic performance initiatives or improve practices or methods.

When this department was established, results-focused measurements indicated that our education system had begun to decline. That information somehow justified our incredibly top-heavy bureaucracy, the implication being that it would reverse the slide into mediocrity. Although several equally unsuccessful reforms followed, none diminished the government's enthusiasm for more. Here they are chronologically.[21]

1. 1989: National Council of Teachers of Mathematics publishes "Curriculum and Evaluation Standards for School

Mathematics." This reformed mathematics education to study concepts rather than specific equations and algorithms.

2. 1990: Carl D. Perkins Vocational and Applied Technologies Act mandated federal funding schools at all levels to work toward preparing students for a technologically oriented future in the workplace.

3. 1994: Educate America Act (Goals 2000) required individual states to submit applications describing how they would create a school improvement program, and make sub-grants to local schools. It set several nationwide goals for schools to reach by the year 2000.

4. 1994: Improve America's Schools Act reauthorized the Elementary and Secondary Education Act of 1965, adding a heavy emphasis on low-income schools.

5. 2001: No Child Left Behind Act required annual standardized testing for students nationwide, grades 3-8.

6. 2006: Carl D. Perkins Vocational and Applied Technologies Act reauthorized the previous act of 1990. It also strengthened the connection between primary and secondary education.

7. 2009: American Recovery and Reinvestment Act allocated over 100 billion dollars in funding toward k-12 educational institutions.

8. 2011: Race to the Top Fund prompted competitive education standards between schools. Finishing the "Race to the Top" at number one meant the school received a much more lucrative grant. This was judged state by state.

9. 2013: Common Core has been described as the most complete overhaul of the education system in United States history and it was never tested before implementation.

The UN's Version of Human Rights

Countless articles and books discuss the type of threat that a federal system of standards poses for the freedoms our current education system enjoys. Let's begin with the United Nations' Universal Declaration of Human Rights (UDHR).

December 10, 1948 marked the day the United Nations adopted this document, which Eleanor Roosevelt championed. The UN developed the UDHR to address the experiences of the Second World War and, as such, it represents the first attempt to express a global list of rights of entitlement for all human beings. The full text is published on the United Nations website.

You will soon realize, if you don't know this already, that the "rights" this organization champions can lead only to totalitarian government and slavery, in complete opposition to the tenets set forth in the foundational documents of this country.

Now, it's being taught in our schools, though it is completely antithetical to our own Declaration of Independence and Constitution. A series of UN rights videos form the core of an eight-week study unit in upstate New York fifth-grade classrooms.[22]

Classroom Instruction on Rights

First, on the following page is the "source" sheet for the homework assignment.[23] The paper begins with a justification of the development of the declared rights in question: because people were poor and disadvantaged, they needed help. Then it summarizes the thirty articles of the UDHR, comprehensively defining the conditions of being human in a God-free world. I highlight God's absence because the paper never acknowledges Him. But rights must have a source. In ignoring God, the declaration necessarily empowers another in His place. It points to the government as granting the delineated rights, indicating that the government is acknowledged as the ultimate power.

A worksheet accompanied the assignment, and read, in part, "No distinction shall be made on the basis of political, jurisdictional or national status of the country or territory to which a person belongs..." The underlying premise of equality between all countries cannot explain the great inequities of opportunity, provision and material success between North and South Korea. If all countries are equal, why did the Soviet Union fall, after receiving massive amounts of charity from the USA for decades? (And, if they are equal, why did they need charity?)

The Universal Declaration of Human Rights

Rights for all members of the human family were first articulated in 1948 in the United Nations' Universal Declaration of Human Rights (UDHR). Following the horrific experiences of the Holocaust and World War II, and amid the grinding poverty of much of the world's population, many people sought to create a document that would capture the hopes, aspirations, and protections to which every person in the world was entitled and ensure that the future of humankind would be different. See Part V, "Appendices," for the complete text and a simplified version of the UDHR.

The 30 articles of the Declaration together form a comprehensive statement covering economic, social, cultural, political, and civil rights. The document is both universal (it applies to all people everywhere) and indivisible (all rights are equally important to the full realization of one's humanity). A *declaration*, however, is not a treaty and lacks any enforcement provisions. Rather it is a statement of intent, a set of principles to which United Nations *member states* commit themselves in an effort to provide all people a life of human dignity.

Over the past 50 years the Universal Declaration of Human Rights has acquired the status of *customary international law* because most states treat it as though it were law. However, governments have not applied this customary law equally. Socialist and communist countries of Eastern Europe, Latin America, and Asia have emphasized social welfare rights, such as education, jobs, and health care, but often have limited the political rights of their citizens. The United States has focused on political and civil rights and has advocated strongly against regimes that torture, deny religious freedom, or persecute minorities. On the other hand, the US government rarely recognizes health care, homelessness, environmental pollution, and other social and economic concerns as human rights issues, especially within its own borders.

Across the USA, a movement is rising to challenge this narrow definition of human rights and to restore social, economic, and cultural rights to their rightful place on the human rights agenda. The right to eat is as fundamental as the right not to be tortured or jailed without charges!

Source: Adapted from Pam Costain, "Moving the Agenda Forward," *Connection to the Americas* 14.8 (October 1997): 4.

Countries weren't created equal; countries were created by men. America, blessed with an understanding of Judeo-Christian principles, began as a great experiment. The founders proposed the principles, "conceived in liberty and dedicated to the proposition that all men are created equal," as Abraham Lincoln eloquently stated in his Gettysburg Address. He didn't mention countries being equal, because they're not.

In all history, no other country has experienced such an incredible explosion of prosperity. This phenomenon resulted from entrepreneurial Americans exercising their *freedom*. For comparison, consider that Europe in the 1600s and 1700s was much wealthier and more advanced than the people in the US, who were virtually camping out in the American wilderness. However, within two hundred years, not only did we catch up with our European cousins, we surpassed them. The only explanation for this was the ability by self-governed US citizens to unleash their human potential, to own the fruits of their dreams, brainpower, will, and labor. That is what we call the American dream.

Countries are *not* equal. There exist dictatorships and monarchies, brutally repressive regimes, as well as governments offering more freedom. But the UN's teaching has infiltrated our schools to dissuade us from that belief.

It has, instead, given our children a dilemma to solve: Who will enforce those thirty articles or rights, and how?

One hotly debated right is the right to life. Some call it a *choice* (of the stronger over the weaker) and others call it an inviolable right. In either instance, it's a situation where the government exerts its ability to legislate.

What other countries can you think of that might try to avoid granting those rights of Article 14, the right to seek asylum? Can the UN bend them to do its will?

> Article 16.
> *(1) Men and women of full age, without any limitation due to race, nationality or religion, have the right to marry and to found a family. They are entitled to equal rights as to marriage, during marriage and at its dissolution.*

> *(2) Marriage shall be entered into only with the free and full consent of the intending spouses.*
> *(3) The family is the natural and fundamental group unit of society and is entitled to protection by society and the State.*[24]

Marriage definitions present another case of debate and divided opinions. For millennia the institution of marriage has been a predominantly religious and cultural one, as opposed to political or fiscal, but this document changes that with its loose reference to "full age," be it six, twelve, sixteen or older. Saudi Arabia has no legal lower age-limit for a girl to be married. In our country, we typically show concern for females' equal rights - more evidence that all countries are not equal.

The document also states, "No one shall be arbitrarily deprived of his property." Define *arbitrarily*.

Americans ought to reject capricious and pernicious policies like these. Americans never voted on them, yet we find ourselves strangely bound by them because they are taught in our schools. What better way to accomplish an agenda than to immerse the young children in it? This should spark great concern for any parent who values the American way of life.

I've saved the best for last:

> Article 25.
> *"Everyone has the right to a standard of living adequate for the health and well-being of himself and of his family, including food, clothing, housing and medical care..."* [25]

Define *adequate*! Define *medical care!* Define *family*! In certain cultures *family* may well be defined as a man and twenty-nine wives, twice as many (or more) parents-in-law, grandparents, and all his offspring. Don't think this isn't within the realm - our Supreme Court just defined marriage simply as two humans who wish to be married to each other. Why the (now) completely arbitrary figure of two. Why not three, or six?

Now, consider that enforcing this "right" necessarily enslaves those who provide those benefits of food, housing, medical care, etc. "Give me my food! It's my *right*!"

Slavery:
1. drudgery, toil
2. submission to a dominating influence
3. a : the state of a person who is a chattel of another
b : the practice of slaveholding[26]

This conjures up images of Mammy sewing Scarlett's dresses. By the way, good luck on the heart surgery your *slave* is performing on you. Your slave of a doctor certainly hopes that goes well.

These positive rights, fully enforced, would precipitate enormous division and resentment among people. Farmers would just sleep in, refusing to grow crops to feed others who don't know how to farm, because there is no pride of workmanship for a slave — when the results of his labor are given to people who did nothing in return for receiving those goods. In fact, we have tremendous examples of the failure of forced labor under communism. Yet this is being taught in American schools.

The dire *consequences* of forced labor won't be discussed with children in school, because the agenda is simply to inspire in them an envy of others, and disdain for themselves. There's no other logically arguable purpose for teaching the UDHR and almost completely neglecting the people and events of our own country's great legacy.

Our children are being taught an enormous lie — the document itself is untrue — *those rights do not exist.* But that its instruction is Common Core aligned is the truth, and its attempt to eclipse our US founding documents is obvious.

One young fifth grader, Gwendolynn Britt, brought home her aced exam, which included this answer:

"Human rights are rights articulated by the government to uphold this country in shape. These rules are inalienable.

They protect our country. The human rights are one of the most important rights ever. I think they hold this country together."[27]

The teacher gave full credit for a response that, overlooking the tragic grammar and obvious misconceptions, blatantly contradicts the Declaration of Independence, which maintains that individual rights derive from God, not government.

If rights derive from the government, Government must provide them and can reasonably take them away — the government gives and the government takes away.

If the UN's supplants our God-given rights, then when the IRS targets private citizens because of their political beliefs, it's not only a reasonable act, but a necessary one. Relinquishing our Constitution and Bill of Rights forfeits the individual's sovereignty, renouncing the ability to question an authority that gives us the right to life, health, food, clothing and happiness, among countless other UN-designated "human rights."

This power raises the government to the level of a deity, one *uncontrolled by any checks and balances*. The elite at the top dictate their wishes, operating without restraints, fulfilling the adage that, "power tend to corrupt and absolute power corrupts absolutely." [28] That kind of deity is, typically, petty and cruel, as well as controlling and vindictive.

In summary, when rights are positive, meaning they are rights to tangible items, someone (i.e. the government) is obliged to supply them and therefore allowed to control them. Our US founding documents purposely turned that idea on its head by proposing that rights can only be guaranteed as negative rights — life, liberty, and pursuit of virtue or happiness. God-given negative rights are things I already have unless someone takes them away from me.

1. Life: I have life, but not the right to protection. I obtain that for myself.

2. Liberty: I begin with freedom, and if others take that from me, it's called slavery, and it's wrong. (More on slave history of the US, later.
3. Pursuit of Happiness: Everything else that I desire I may attempt to obtain, as long as I don't infringe on the first two rights of others.
4. There isn't a number four! The rest are privileges! Food doesn't magically appear, so I must procure it for myself, legally, because I have no inherent *right* to it. It is a benefit I may *earn*, or receive *voluntarily* from someone else. And to my eternal dismay, I may not compel Jimmy Choo to produce fabulous shoes for me in my size, simply by claiming they are my *right*.

COMMON CORE

~

"I have never let my schooling interfere with my education."
~ Mark Twain[29]

Common Core recycles a decades-old, top-down approach to education clearly laid out in a letter sent to Hillary Clinton by Marc Tucker, president of the National Center on Education and the Economy (NCEE), immediately after Bill Clinton's 1992 presidential victory. Marc Tucker has and is now advising the Obama Administration's U. S. Department of Education about how to implement the Common Core Standards and Race to the Top programs.

Marc Tucker and Hillary Clinton apparently had plans to have national standards, national tests, national curriculum, and a national database way back in the 1980's.

The "Dear Hillary" letter, written on Nov. 11, 1992 by Marc Tucker, lays out a plan "to remold the entire American system" into "a seamless web that literally extends from cradle to grave and is the same system for everyone," coordinated by "a system of labor market boards at the local, state and federal levels" where curriculum and "job matching" will be handled by counselors "accessing the integrated computer-based program." [30]

Many people have passionate opinions about Common Core, and I'm no different. To those who inquire about my viewpoint, I wish I could say, "Drink plenty of fluids, get lots of rest, and it will go away in a few days."

Unfortunately, that won't work, on several levels. I must point out here that although the fight against Common Core still rages and many battles have been 'won,' the textbooks have already been changed, the teachers taught the new strategies and standards, and therefore, Common Core is here to stay in most of our schools today, if perhaps eventually by another name. For this reason, I include here a comprehensive discussion of the failings of Common Core, which, by its very existence, impugns the virtue of our Department of Education, *down to its core.*

What is Common Core?

- Designed primarily by non-educators, it's the biggest overhaul of the education system, ever.
- Forty-five states adopted it *before it was written* because of the money promised by the federal Race to the Top funding.
- Its implementation sets a dangerous precedent, sacrificing state sovereignty to the federal government, which takes away the autonomy of school boards, parents, and teachers.
- This outrageously constructed plan prohibits any amendments or changes.
- In California alone, for the mind-boggling amount of $12-30 billion, it fixes nothing, improves nothing, but institutes lower standards than 1997.
- Yet it requires data tracking—400 data points—on all children, making kids across the nation DC's Guinea pigs.
- And, it's already in our schools.

Proponents argue that Common Core isn't a curriculum. Rather, it's a set of standards for educational goals, which should provide a more homogenous learning experience for students. With Common Core's expected level of standardization, students who move from one community to another may expect the same education - the same subjects, covering the same materials, taught in the same way - in their new school, that they were receiving in the old one.

But is homogeneity a good thing?

The implication is that MacDonald's is great because you can count on them to provide the same burger in every state, wherever you find a franchise. Then again, sometimes you might want a taco.

Reducing the debate to those particulars leads to a hollow assumption, because Common Core involves changing the *way* things are taught. Admittedly, proponents argue they're *improving* the way things are taught. At the same time, they insist that it's only standards, not curricula.

Complicated and Confusing

Common Core insists on teaching young children very complicated ways to solve multiplication problems that older generations performed with the simpler standard algorithm. It proposes postponing the traditional, easy-to-understand method until later grades. Making math more difficult can easily cause children to give up on it at an early age. It can give them the impression that they aren't smart. It can prejudice them against math.

The best example of this is using addition to solve a subtraction problem. The standard algorithm is based on understanding of the nature of numbers and their relationships. Here's an example:

Standard algorithm:

$$\begin{array}{r} 368 \\ \underline{-47} \\ 321 \end{array}$$

8-7=1, 6-4=2, and 3-0=3.

With time-tested practice of borrowing, and by relying on our base-ten numerical system, the standard algorithm is the simplest, most straightforward method for understanding and engaging the concept of subtraction for multi-digit numbers: break them into their digits and place-values, and proceed.

Common Core method:

Subtract 47 from 368 by counting up.

47
+3 Count up to the nearest 10.
50
+50 Count up to the nearest 100.
100
+200 Count up to the largest possible hundred.
300
+68 Count up to the number.
368

Then add the 'count up' numbers all together to see how much you added, total, to find the *difference*:

3 + 50 + 200 + 68 = 321

You counted up by 321, so 368 - 47 = 321.

Rather than encouraging interest and achievement, the new system dissuades students from pursuing math by complicating it beyond their comprehension. This phenomenon is best illustrated with the Common Core's promotion of the "lattice" method.

Lattice Method:

STEP 1

To multiply using the lattice method, create a grid with diagonal lines and write in the numbers to be multiplied. The multiplicand will read across the top of the grid, in the column headers, and the multiplier will read down the right side of the grid.

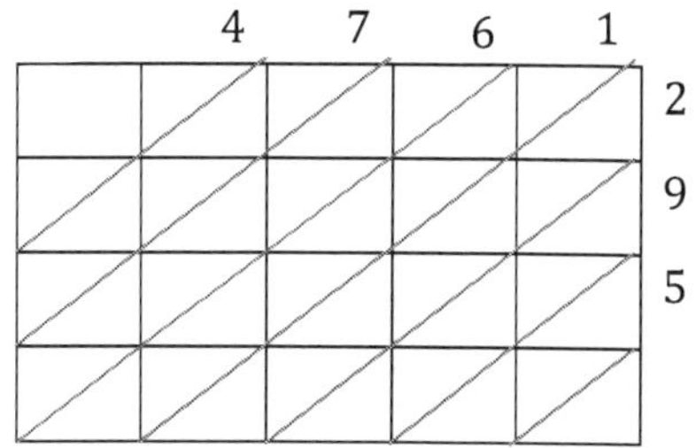

Please note that this is counter-intuitive, and forces the student to work backwards (to the left) as they work the problem down.

STEP 2

After drawing in diagonal lines throughout the grid, multiply each column by each row, splitting two-digit products to either side of the diagonal in the corresponding box on the grid. Note how the place values become obscured.

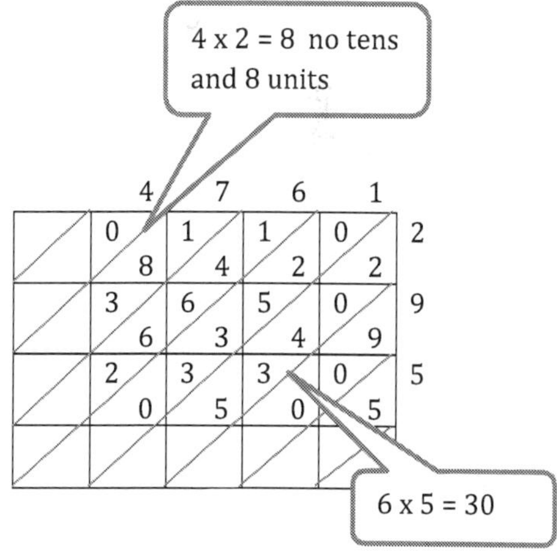

STEP 3

Add the diagonals to get each answer and place the corresponding sums in the final diagonal spaces along the bottom and left sides of the grid. For carries, mark the carry-over at the top of the next diagonal.

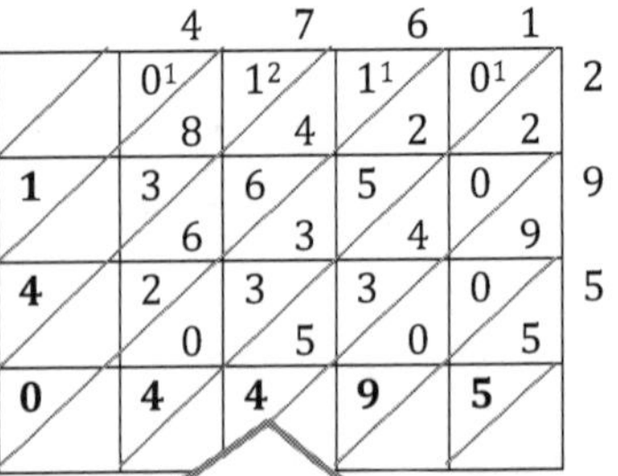

2 + 0 + 4 + 3 + 5 = 14. Mark the four at the bottom; carry the one into the top of the next diagonal at the top.

STEP 4

The answer may be derived by reading the far left column as it wraps around along the bottom.

Note how much like magic this process is, how difficult it is to check the work, and how children must be very talented at keeping their numbers and grids neat!

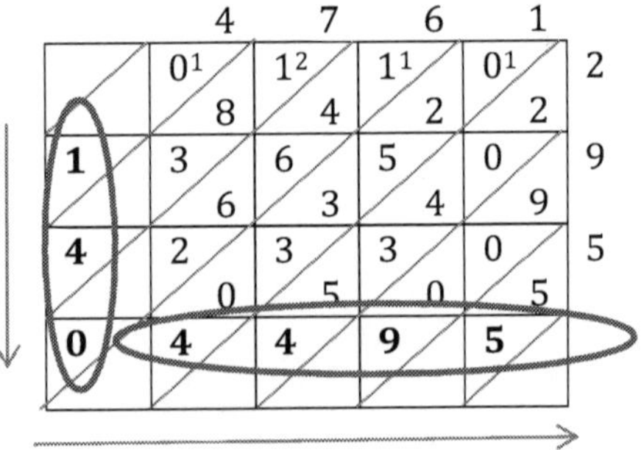

The Product = 1,404,496

If a fourth-grader botches the lines just a bit, she gets the wrong answer. It's like *magic math*. While I love math games and similar fun things, this method actually complicates otherwise simple concepts. The goal of any math program, especially for younger children, should be to make the concepts easy to understand, not nearly impossible.

Some might argue that "carrying" is more difficult than this method, which often (but not always) avoids it. That contradicts the fundamentals of how our base-10 mathematical system works. *Lattice inhibits the student's understanding of mathematics.*

Untested, yet Accepted

There exists no reasonable common sense explanation for the shift to more complicated, more confusing math methods, except to make children quit trying. In addition, the unfamiliar new algorithms, lattice method, adding up, and others, will likely frustrate parents. Also, the additional burden on teachers has precipitated a postponement of algebra from eighth to ninth grade for most students.

Many other examples of the perverted methods taught under Common Core exist — too many to cover here. Understand that Common Core is *completely* untested with *no* evidence it will improve performance or skills. No data supports the assertion that implementing Common Core will result in "Preparing America's Students for College and Career." [31]

No one tested the standards because states adopted them even before they were written. Why would anyone with common sense vote this way? You wouldn't pay a contractor before he completes the project. Nor would you compensate him before he even submits his proposal! That would be foolish. And yet, that's what has happened here—with your tax dollars.

Dr. Sandra Stotsky wrote, "The development of the standards *violated* almost every civic procedure that I have been familiar with in my life and I have been in the master's department of Education in charge of the public process for the development of our standards so I know what the public process is like from a department of education point of view." [32] (Emphasis mine.)

Why would the creators/proponents of Common Core want to dumb down our children? This difficult question suggests a disturbing answer.

Smarter customers demand better service. Dumbed-down people become more reliant on government, another way to ensure job security for bureaucrats.

APUSH drama

Recently, Common Core revamped the requirements, or standards, for Advanced Placement United States History (APUSH). While nine members of the College Board's Advanced

Placement United States History Curriculum Development and Assessment Committee take credit for authorship of the APUSH Curriculum Framework, fifty-five lauded scholars denounced the revisionist and flawed approach of the progressive's new history curriculum, ostensibly because of their tremendous bias against the US democracy and for progressive totalitarianism. Here are just a few of them:

> *11. Although George Washington's Farewell Address warned about the dangers of divisive political parties and permanent foreign alliances... (Page 43. This is the Framework's sole reference to George Washington.)*
>
> *12. The colonists' belief in the superiority of republican self-government based on the natural rights of the people found its clearest American expression in Thomas Paine's Common Sense and in the Declaration of Independence. (Page 43. This is the Framework's sole reference to the Declaration of Independence. Note that it actually follows Washington's Farewell Address. Although the Framework stresses the skill of historical causation, the document contains numerous examples of events that are not presented in chronological order.)*
>
> *15. Resistance to initiatives for democracy and inclusion included proslavery arguments, rising xenophobia, antiblack sentiments in political and popular culture, and restrictive anti-Indian policies. (Page 49. Note that the Framework omits both Jeffersonian and Jacksonian democracy. This biased statement reinforces the Framework's consistently negative portrayal of the American experience.)*
>
> *17. The idea of Manifest Destiny, which asserted U.S. power in the Western Hemisphere and supported U.S. expansion westward, was built on a belief in white racial superiority and a sense of American cultural superiority, and helped to shape the era's political debates. (Page 54. Note that generations of American students have been taught that Manifest Destiny expressed America's mission*

to spread its democratic institutions and technology across the continent. This revisionist definition clearly expresses the Framework's negative biases.)

27. Teachers have the flexibility to use examples such as the following: Students for a Democratic Society, Black Panthers. (Page 74. Note that the Framework omits Rosa Parks and Dr. King, but does have room for the SDS and the Black Panthers.)

28. President Ronald Reagan, who initially rejected détente with increased defense spending, military action, and bellicose rhetoric, later developed a friendly relationship with Soviet leader Mikhail Gorbachev, leading to significant arms reductions by both countries. (Page 78. Note that this is the Framework's simplistic explanation for how and why the Cold War ended.)[33]

Upon his review, Peter Wood, President of the National Association of scholars, wrote, "In view of the many, many faults in American K-12 education, should the College Board's hapless revision of the Advanced Placement framework in American history occasion special concern? My answer is a qualified yes. There are bigger problems, but this is one of those small problems that signifies larger things. Our national memory is slipping."[34]

Jane Robbins (senior fellow at the American Principles Project) and Larry Krieger (a retired AP U.S. history teacher) posted an article, "New Advanced Placement Framework Distorts America's History."[35] Krieger also issued a follow-up piece titled, "Yes, the New AP Framework Does Distort U.S. History."[36]

Wood summarized some of their objections, with which he agrees, that the revised standards "advance a negative view of America."

The College Board responded to critics by issuing a statement, part of which read, "At the root of current objections to this highly regarded process is a blatant disregard for the facts," the statement said. "The College Board will not compromise the integrity of the Advanced Placement Program."[37] In a separate letter,[38] they also argued that the omissions of Reverend Doctor

Martin Luther King, Thomas Jefferson and Benjamin Franklin were simply because the teacher would obviously include them anyway. Other seminal American documents are also absent. For instance, the Mayflower Compact, Lincoln's Gettysburg Address, and John F. Kennedy's Inaugural Address are universally considered uniquely American. Their exclusion begs the question of the necessity of standards that seem designed to obscure rather than highlight American excellence.

When is a standard not a standard?

Of the new standards, Daniel Henninger of the Wall Street Journal wrote, "The original AP U.S. history guidelines were a case study in the left's irrepressible impulse, here or elsewhere, to always go too far."[39]

The Republican National Committee called for a delay of implementation.[40] Oklahoma Legislators moved to cut funding for APUSH [41] Suffice it to say that with such controversy surrounding the standards, something needed to be done to appease the critics, and something was. They were revamped, under protest.

Perhaps the College Board isn't as concerned about its integrity as the money it generates. Suffice it to say that we've now seen the teeth of this beast, it has shown its intentions, and we should not be lulled into complacency but a small concession.

Re-right-ing

"If your friend lied to you once, would you take everything they said afterwards with a grain of salt? Would you think for a moment (or more) about the things they had said in the past, rehashing how those had turned out, if they had ended up being true or false, if there were consequences that you might have avoided had you known your friend was lying? Someone who blatantly lies puts a pall over everything they claim after that, and their entire person becomes suspect, at least to a discerning, honest individual.

Unfortunately, lying is commonplace today. Holding people accountable has become tantamount to racism, sexism, discrimination, and is usually the first accusation liars resort to when confronted with their lies.

But "the truth is a very narrow path, stupidity a never ending jungle," Johan Wolfgang Von Goethe assures us. This makes it all the more disconcerting when educational institutions caught in a lie excuse it by admitting it isn't the only lie they're telling. Perhaps they're using a "new math" to insist that two wrongs do make a right.

Denton, Texas uses the textbook *United States History: Preparing for the Advanced Placement Examination* that incorrectly summarizes the second amendment: *The people have the right to keep and bear arms in a state militia.*

Here's the correct quote:

> *Amendment* II: *A well-regulated militia, being necessary to the security of a free state, the right of the people to keep and bear arms, shall not be infringed.*

This single egregious misstatement is serious enough to warrant expulsion of the book from their roster, when many good textbooks are available that teach the truth. Their excuse is that the Denton Independent School District maintains they only use the book as "supplemental" material and they are "disseminating the correct information on the Second Amendment" from other texts.[42]

So, they choose to keep the lie and muddy the water. This serves only to confuse students. My intense feelings about this cut to the very core of what's wrong with our educational system: political correctness, or the inability to *discern*.

The school's protest that the book is *supplemental* is embarrassingly stupid and disingenuous. There aren't two versions of truth. Logic compels us to agree that only one is true. The other is a lie, has no positive value, and because it necessarily misleads, should be thrown out. Poop in the water, as I say.

It's important to figure out *why* the book misquotes the second amendment. I doubt it was an accident. A careless mistake is quite unlikely. Changing copy from a historical document is *purposeful.* However, if enough people are persuaded to believe a lie, then the truth may be ignored. (For example, when Weapons of Mass Destruction (WMD) in Iraq were previously documented — Saddam Hussein used them on his own subjects — but subsequently never actually found, they were incorrectly determined to *be* and to *have been* nonexistent. That *lie* was repeated so frequently, it now masquerades as truth to those who lack discernment, regardless of the WMD's later discovery.)[43]

In a further review of the book, authored by Dr. John Newman and Dr. John Schmalbach, The Blaze also discovered a potentially controversial passage on the American Revolution. The text asks: "The Revolution—Radical or Conservative?"[44]

The authors of the questionable textbook call those who fought in the Revolutionary War "revolutionary mobs" and "American mobs."

> *"In comparing the three revolutions, a few historians have concentrated on the actions of revolutionary mobs, such as the American Sons of Liberty. Again, there are two divergent interpretations: (1) the mobs in all three countries engaged in the same radical activities, and (2) the American mobs had a much easier time of it than the French and Russian mobs, who encountered ruthless repression by military authorities."*

Views of Revolution

This distortion implies that the American revolutionaries had an easy time of battling the greatest military force in the world. It sounds like those "divergent interpretations" originate with those same authors. Significantly, how are these interpretations, which are less *divergent* than *independent,* at all *relevant*? Those questions don't interest the educators who promote this text. It would be more instructive and beneficial to ask how these revolutions differed in their origins and outcomes, which would lead to an examination of those qualities, views and actions which made America unique and great.

In summary, what we have here is an attempt to equate the American revolutionaries with mercenary or radical mob elements who would seek to topple their own government. The lesson for children studying from this text is that government should not be questioned.

The American Revolution was exceptional because the people fought for freedom *from* tyranny and *for* a government of the people, by the people, and for the people. The proof is clear, in that America quickly became the world's superpower, a beacon on a hill. Other revolutions and mob actions, such as the French revolution, can make no such claims.

We are engaged in a battle for truth against those who would mutate it into lies to serve their perverse political agendas. It is as simple as freedom versus slavery, democracy versus communism, right versus wrong. The irony here is that to win, the authors and their supporters must also lose in this ages-old battle.

If no sacrifice is noble, if our founding fathers were not exceptional, if our country should not stand as a shining city on the hill for freedom in the storms of dictatorships and tyranny, then there's no moral superiority, no right, no wrong, and no truth.

If the second amendment doesn't specifically protect the individual from his government, but simply recommends the state militia have arms, we succumb to the government as slaves and let it grow in oppressive control at our expense. That's the legacy in history that our founders sought, and succeeded, for a time, to change.

George Orwell said, "Who controls the past controls the future. Who controls the present controls the past." Our educators should know this. They should stop rewriting history, or, ultimately, they'll destine us all to repeat it.

The US and Slavery

It's long been taught, sometimes simply by omission, that the founders were all white men who either owned slaves or condoned the practice—a drastic and destructive fabrication. George Washington received his slaves when he was fourteen, in

Virginia, a state where it was *illegal to release them*. Yes, you read that correctly. At that time it was *against the law* to set slaves free.

In fact, the original versions of our founding documents were strongly worded against slavery. However, the founders knew that they needed support from all the states in order to repel Great Britain, the world's greatest military power of the day. Thomas Jefferson, who drafted the original Declaration of Independence, included a full paragraph deriding the slave trade and King George's part in it, but his indictment offended colonists who owned slaves. As he contended in later writings, delegates from South Carolina and Georgia, as well as northern merchants who profited from the slave trade, insisted on removing most of it. Here is the original language.

> *He [King George] has waged cruel war against human nature itself, violating its most sacred rights of life and liberty in the persons of a distant people who never offended him, captivating & carrying them into slavery in another hemisphere or to incur miserable death in their transportation thither. This piratical warfare, the opprobrium of infidel powers, is the warfare of the Christian King of Great Britain. Determined to keep open a market where Men should be bought & sold, he has prostituted his negative for suppressing every legislative attempt to prohibit or restrain this execrable commerce. And that this assemblage of horrors might want no fact of distinguished die, he is now exciting those very people to rise in arms among us, and to purchase that liberty of which he has deprived them, by murdering the people on whom he has obtruded them: thus paying off former crimes committed again the Liberties of one people, with crimes which he urges them to commit against the lives of another.*[45]

The founders postponed the fight over slavery in order to win their fight for independence. While we can debate the prudence of that delay, we shouldn't succumb to the erroneous belief that our founders all condoned slavery as part of the economic system. It was a worldwide human condition and had been for man thought history. Although it wasn't even invented in the Americas, the US is the only country in the world that expended tremendous blood and treasure to free slaves and abolish the practice here.

Finally, even if the founders had agreed to immediately emancipate all the slaves, they had no practical way to do so. It would have meant taking an entire group of people who had only known dependence and thrusting them into new circumstances with little societal support. This monumental task was too much for men focused on the challenge of establishing a new nation and breaking ties with the most powerful country in the world.

Sadly, American classrooms conceal these facts to instill the narrative that flawed, bigoted old white men founded our country. Bernie Sanders, the socialist running for the presidency in 2016, said, "I hope that every person in this room today understands that it is unacceptable to judge people, discriminate against people based on the color of their skin. And I will also say, that as a nation — the truth is a nation that in many ways was created, and I'm sorry to have to say this — from way back, on racist principles, that's a fact."[46] It is an old refrain that has now taken root in our education bureaucracy, which engenders fear and anger, as opposed to lauding the great benefits that this country offers its citizens.

Added to the teaching in The Universal Declaration of Human Rights that everyone has rights to food, shelter, new running shoes, etc., this produces disgruntled, resentful students who probably don't even know why they feel violated. When you teach children they have a right to candy, and yet they have none, they're bound to feel cheated. *It's the education system that is robbing them.*

Let's Role the Videotape!

In some classrooms, the eight-week education on UDHR is enhanced with video instruction.[47] To be fair, the Common Core State Standards Initiative (CCSSI) curriculum also provides for a three week course on the original version of our "inalienable rights... endowed by our creator," of "life, liberty and the pursuit of happiness." So, our founders' history-changing declaration is given 3/8ths of the attention of the UN's.

At the end of the initial video, the teachers ask their pupils to sign a declaration of agreement. After a *single* presentation without a dissenting position offered, children are asked to affirm their allegiance to UDHR with their signatures on a petition to implement the UDHR.

It doesn't stop there. Though only eight videos comprise the in-school curriculum, a total of thirty videos are available, designed to cement a view that twists and perverts the concept of human rights found in American founding documents. With no alternative, students' innocent minds accept the lies, which are worse for the intellect than junk food is for the body. The indoctrination begins at an early age when they are most receptive to information from authority figures. Parents, either too busy or disinterested to analyze the values their kids are being taught, are caught off guard, believing that schools impartially teach information. They often remain unaware that the entitled attitude their kids bring home emanates directly from classroom instruction.

Also of interest: the Church of Scientology produces all the videos in the course. Are they a reliable source for your child's education?

Little Jimmy Feels Cheated

Jimmy is taught that clothing and shelter are human rights and he lives in a one-bedroom cold-water flat with his mom, who shops at thrift stores and works two minimum-wage part-time jobs. His friend Cooper lives in a nice three-bedroom house with a swing-set and wears the most popular jeans and sneakers. What might Jimmy conclude about the differences in their situations? With biased information and little skill in reasoning, he might think this way.

> *We both have the same rights, because we're equal, so we should both have the same clothing and homes, because they're human rights, which we're entitled to have. I want a*

nice bedroom, clothes, and a backyard like Cooper has. But the system cheated my mom even though we all deserve to be treated equally. Why do we have so much less? Mom must be stupid or she was tricked. I feel sorry for her. When I grow up I'm gonna make sure the system pays me back with even more for not taking care of us properly now.

Kids grow up disgruntled with little or no understanding why they have these feelings, and lack the ability to analyze them objectively. Anger stifles them, and then becomes a crutch, an excuse, and a liability.

Increasingly larger government thrives on this dynamic, because ultimately, government needs dependency to remain relevant. Without additional dependency, our government would cease to grow. Ask the logical question. "Do we have enough laws?"

Big government responds, "Absolutely not!"

A free, independent people avoid government's involvement in their lives, but a dependent people have no choice. They come to rely on it, even welcome it, despite the massive evidence of disastrous results.

An Informational Meeting

On May second, 2013, in Cape Girardeau, the Department of Elementary and Secondary Education of Missouri held informational meetings "to answer questions related to the State Board of Education's decision in 2010 to adopt new standards in English language arts and mathematics, more commonly known as the Common Core State Standards."[48]

One event was at the Career and Technology Center. Brian Bollmann attended and reported back. He focused on how the organizers of the meeting controlled messaging and divided the attendees, making sure that proponents of Common Core were seated at each table to 'facilitate' (read *control*) the conversation.

The organizers forbade the free exchange of questions and ideas with the representatives of Common Core on the dais. This came as no surprise to Mr. Bollmann because in his opinion, *Common Core is all about control.* Informational meetings create the illusion that participants have input, while they are stealthily prevented from contributing. Through Mr. Bollmann's report, we can surmise the divide-and-conquer method proved quite effective. What struck me was this final revelation:

> *At a Table #12 side discussion, a teacher stated that she liked Common Core because every school would teach the same topics at the same grade levels. She continued that children moving state-to-state would be able to pick right up where they left off in their new school.*
>
> *Her statement helped me finally crystallize my foremost reason for opposing it. CCSSI removes any desire for one school to work to excel. Children will be tested for certain skills at certain ages, and there will actually be negative reinforcement should a school decide to teach subjects at different grade levels to help them excel.*[49]

Boy, it's a good thing that all children are exactly alike! Just stick them on the assembly line, and input the appropriate data as they go. They will all learn at the same pace with the same materials, and achieve the same results. (Note: sarcasm.)

Rotting from the Head

~

"I know no safe depositary of the ultimate powers of the society but the people themselves; and if we think them not enlightened enough to exercise their control with a wholesome discretion, the remedy is not to take it from them, but to inform their discretion by education. This is the true corrective of abuses of constitutional power."

~ Thomas Jefferson to W. Jarvis, 1820[50]

The Great Experiment

The United States was founded as a great experiment. Fittingly, each state served as its own proving ground, like a Petri dish growing ideas and testing strategies. This was the founders' vision of promoting freedom and advancing humanity. This system encouraged people to seek the best solutions and policies, and, by default, discouraged the less successful ones. And so, the founders harnessed the benefits of competition.

For this reason, the states maintained sovereignty of every power not specifically assigned by the Constitution to the federal government. An added benefit of that construct was the limitations on the potential growth of federal power. Our forefathers understood that government works best when kept close to home. It expected each state to find its own way and make the best choices for its citizens. This kept the bar of achievement high.

Now that bar has been artificially lowered and the question is how to raise it again. By establishing a federal agency for education, US citizens lost much of their power. The stated goal of homogeneity betrays with definitive finality a basic foundational tenet of our country — that free-market competition encourages all to thrive. If all the states have the same standards, how can we measure how good they are? Worse, what motivates them to excel? The end result must necessarily be that all participants perform equally *poorly*.

Common Sense and Choices

Wendy's ran a commercial many years ago. A stocky, elderly woman in a hair net and gray sack dress walked on a catwalk, like a clumsy model, in corrective orthotic shoes.

The fashion show broadcaster announced, in a heavy Russian accent, "Dehy-veer!" (Day wear.) In the next segment, she held a beach ball, sashaying, albeit frumpily, down the runway, to the pronouncement, "Shvim-veer!" (Swim wear) by the announcer.

Wendy's wanted to emphasize their choices for people—that customers could order burgers exactly the way they wanted them.

In the final image, which I unfortunately can't get out of my mind, the model (and I use that term loosely) displayed a bland, yet oddly superior expression as she walked toward the camera brandishing a long, silver, illuminated flashlight. "Eef-ning-veer!" (Evening wear.)

Competition is good. Choice is good. Children aren't just alike and their education programs shouldn't be identical. Because the schools are run by a bureaucracy and controlled in a large part by the unions, they discard choice for a supposedly easier one-size-fits-all approach. This squelches motivation, keeping kids from stepping outside the status quo and discouraging the urge to excel.

Brian Bollmann noted that they face reprisals for atypical behavior. Children hear this message: *Stay at your grade level with everyone else. Excellence will not be tolerated.*

Homogeneity is prized over individualism; it's easier to predict and control, especially in a bureaucracy.

Removing the desire to excel contains a frightening resemblance to shaping students into good little communists. Some advocates for Common Core might take exception to my assessment and prediction of outcomes that follow implementation of CCSS. Granted, while not all proponents are Marxists, that doesn't affect the logic or results.

The greatest goal of a solid education is to give students the ability to think, to reason, and to discern. Disciplines like algebra and writing are simply the tools for greater goals. For instance, mathematics exposes a student to rudimentary logic. Persuasive writing teaches students how to structure a logical argument, stimulating development of their skills of analysis and reason. If the only focus is to fill each student with facts, without teaching them to think, they'll grow bored and lose interest. Unfortunately, that appears to be the strategy of these new standards.

I recently took part in a forum on Common Core, hosted by our local newspaper, with representatives in attendance for both sides of the issue. I was astonished to hear our Superintendent of Schools say, "I'm not sure learning long division is even all that necessary anymore. These kids will always have calculators."

He clearly didn't comprehend that learning long division is more about learning the manipulation of numbers, the implementation of formula, and the comprehension of relationships. Without overstating this, long division is far more than simply finding the answers to a plethora of math problems, all of which, of course, could be done by a calculator.

Despite his lofty title, his attitude was antithetical to the basic tenets of education. For that matter, the logical conclusion of his approach to education would mean the only learning necessary for any child would be to perfect a specific skill in order to fill a job after graduation. *Job preparedness, indeed.*

The skills emphasized are narrowly focused to prepare students for college and/or prepare them for a particular career. This is the Common Core mantra. Learn to hold a job or do rote labor. Don't learn to reason, analyze, and draw conclusions. Do not teach students to *think.*

The event was standing room only and heavily attended by anti-Common Core activists. A rowdy mood permeated the audience, one that clearly felt betrayed by the unilateral implementation of the greatest overhaul of the country's education system—ever. They wanted to be heard, and they were, for a short time.

Toward the end of the forum, when the moderator tried cutting off the question microphones in the audience, a nervous blond woman in front of me walked up and insisted on speaking.

The moderator tried to silence her, saying we'd run out of time, but the audience encouraged him to let her talk—the attendees weren't in any hurry.

She asked about a video that shows a Common Core approved workbook encouraging children to choose the stronger verb, between "Mommy *asks* me to clean my room," and "Mommy *nags* me to clean my room." The correct answer is "nags." She demanded to know why they are bringing this kind of anti-parent teaching into the classroom? And how we could be assured this wouldn't happen in our classrooms?

The Superintendent of Schools answered that we should let the kids decide on what teaching seemed appropriate. *Let the children decide?* Think about what kinds of unguided choices they would make! Most of them would eat M&Ms and watch YouTube videos all day if they were allowed set their own schedules.

One wonders what children he spends time with that would lead him to conclude that kids are capable of demonstrating the foresight and sophistication to select subjects and materials for a good education — that without adult assistance they can look ahead and plan wisely for their yet-to-be-determined lives. These are the same children who recently learned to wash their hands after they wipe themselves.

The superintendent's attitude betrays the very word *education*, which has as its Latin roots *educere,* or "to lead out." He implied that children can generally make better choices than adults, especially in regards to how they refer to adults themselves.

With horrible, telling gaffs like that, it's no wonder the schools had barely invited parents to the forum. It also explains why most parents never heard of CCSSI until it was nearly too late and required appeal instead of simple choice.

Even worse was his misrepresentation of the program he lauded. The standards actually impose *more* constraints on what children learn, not less; it has more fixed directives for the teachers to follow, not less.

"With the Common Core national education

> *standards coming under increased scrutiny from conservative activists, Republican politicians, and even teachers unions, The Daily Caller News Foundation took a look at the Obama administration's recommended reading list for K-12 kids. Common Core's English Standards stress nonfiction over literature: By grade 12, 70 percent of what students read should be informational rather than literary."*[51]

Children like stories; even adults like stories, so it's a rare child who would be enthralled with scientific non-fiction, such as the recommended text *'Invasive Plant Inventory'* by the California Invasive Plant Council. Seriously? A list of invasive plants constitutes educational literature, now? How does this even begin to compete with Great Expectations? Pretty soon they'll change that title to "No Expectations."

By omitting great literature and substituting boring texts, schools necessarily fail to engage students, betraying the supposed promise to inspire lifelong readers and learners. Antithetically, students likely will seek to escape from opportunities to learn, rather than embrace them.

Now, remember that this educator is representative, not simply of Common Core, but the entire public education bureaucracy.

POWER PLAY

~

"It is the mark of an educated mind to be able to entertain a thought without accepting it."
~ Aristotle[52]

When states impose broad new standards in our schools, without any input from educators or parents, and without discussion or a vote, that's a totalitarian act. Parents and school boards that passively accept this sort of infringement on their rights shouldn't be surprised or upset when eventually they're informed that their opinions are unnecessary.

As the forced implementation of this new curriculum already indicates, Common Core is the antithesis of traditional education, which seeks to stimulate the child to discover knowledge and wisdom. It stifles individualism and restricts learning. It's been called behavior modification, brainwashing, even "re-education," but *true* education, it's not.

The best cure for Common Core, which is a name now associated with the entirety of what ails our education system, is to arm parents with accurate information. Once they understand what the government is teaching their children, they may well consider alternatives such as home schooling.

In 2013, I interviewed Charlotte Thomson Iserbyt on my radio show, Flash Point Live. She's an astute and educated woman, with a formidable amount of knowledge. She served as the Senior Policy Advisor at the U.S. Department of Education under Ronald Reagan. While working there, she discovered a long-term strategic plan by tax-exempt foundations and corporations to *transform* America through our education system. Long before it was a familiar term, she became a whistle-blower.

Dumbing Down

Iserbyt lived through WWII, and heard people say things like, “Ending discrimination and changing values are probably *more important than reading* in moving low income families into the middle class.” Some of the main proponents of the movement to dumb down education said these things as a way to create a working class. Hearing this made my heart palpitate.

It’s eerily like the “worker’s paradise” that the Marxist movement promoted. Iserbyt is justified in her skepticism and condemnation of the current efforts for reform in our education system. The disease of achievement reduction has never left the body of our education system. It has only become more and more entrenched.

I say this because President Obama said, “We are five days away from *fundamentally transforming* the United States of America.” What better method to transform fundamentally than to co-opt the hearts and minds of the children of this country? Perhaps this is not proof in and of itself, but please recall the secretive manner in which the shift is occurring.

Forty-five states adopted the new standards *before they were written*. Does this sound like they have your child’s interests at heart? These same states began implementing this fundamental overhaul of our education system without a vote and in secret. The unavoidable conclusion is that those in power didn’t want parents to be aware. They also never asked for any proof that the new standards had any positive effect on education results, but claimed that they were superlative to the old standards. Nancy Pelosi said about Obamacare, “We have to pass the bill to find out what’s in it.” That her statement stood unchallenged by a majority of Americans is, alone, enough to sum up the state of our current, un-thought-provoking education system.

Today, parents must struggle to stay informed. When they ask about curriculum and Common Core, they are placated with slogans. I spoke with two women I met at the park one day. After a bit of conversation, I asked the first if she had heard of Common Core.

She said, "No, what's that?" She was standing next to her good friend, a public school elementary teacher, but had never heard of Common Core, the biggest reform of our US education system ever.

I started to tell her, and the teacher piped up, "I can tell you've heard a lot of the bad rumors about Common Core, but I'm a teacher and there are a lot of really great things about it."

"Really?" I literally couldn't help myself, because her rhetoric sounded canned and dismissive. "Is that why you're moving to Texas, where they've voted its cousin out of the state?" I didn't know if she was hypocritical or just ridiculous. "If it's so great why aren't you staying to teach it, and why hasn't your friend here heard you expounding on its benefits?"

She claimed she was moving out of California to avoid the high taxes. It's an understandable move, because Jerry Brown committed the state to spend $1.5 billion to implement the untried, unproven, and predictably catastrophic CCSSI.

That is one wily teacher!

Illogical Logic

She continued to shrug off the negatives I pointed out, while lauding the standards, and their lofty *goals*. This "reasoning" evidenced another gaping flaw in our public education system—the inability to analyze data and draw reasoned conclusions. "Goals" do not assure *success* (and hope is not a strategy). Her logic — and I use that term hesitantly — followed these lines:

Our education system is failing our kids.

We need to fix the system.

Administrators say new standards will fix it.

Therefore, new standards must be good.

It was clear to me that she'd had a large serving of the punch. To anyone questioning the standards, or lack of proof of their efficacy, or their prohibitive cost, or their dubious origins, the well-trained answer from proponents is, "The new standards are great. Look how much preparation went into them!" Any criticisms are met with, "Not everything is perfect, and these are better than nothing," or, "The good out-weighs the bad." We can call this

"Pelosi logic." Apparently, we have to implement the standards to find out what's in them, or even if they will work.

One last, logical question: if the old standards were so bad that virtually any new standards must be better, who put the old standards in place, and whatever were they thinking? Of course, this is a rhetorical question. And it isn't really about standards.

It's about *control.*

Common Core and Mental Health

Now that Common Core has been implemented, teachers have begun reporting their experiences. After a couple of years' transition to Common Core, it's now in full swing. One dedicated teacher, who works in a school that is supportive of students' education and their dreams for the future, wrote about the expectations for herself and her students. Here are some highlights:

> *"I was told numerous times that if students did not excel, it was that I was failing the student...*
>
> *I was told that I need to challenge students by bringing them to their "frustration level"– that doing so would challenge them to work and that they would rise to the occasion.*
>
> *I envisioned students throwing up their hands in resignation and transforming into behavior problems."*[53]

While she doesn't demonize anyone in her article, she does question Common Core's choice to evaluate teachers based solely on testing - from a curriculum that has never been tested. That sets up a hypocritical situation, where the judgment itself is based on un-judged material. She seems to resent the idea that she is simply *directed,* rather than *consulted* as a seasoned professional.

> *"I understand that this is the nature of top-down 'leadership.' The only one with the freedom is the one at the*

very top. All others have some consequence, the outcome of which they seek to determine by controlling the actions of those lower than them in the chain. So I understand why my district is so prescriptive in telling me as an English teacher the specific literature I am to use and why my school administration is telling me not only what to teach but how to teach it, down to the exact lesson template. They are grasping for control."[54] (Emphasis mine.)

Telling, isn't it? And infuriating, too.

Because of the ridiculous expectations placed on both teachers and children, by myriad non-professionals who crafted and directed Common Core, the author predicts that the number one 21st century job will be that of a mental health counselor. That sounds about right.

Poop in the Water

~

"Education is the ability to listen to almost anything without losing your temper or your self-confidence."
~ Robert Frost[55]

It's a hot, sunny day and you're thirsty. I graciously present you with a pristine glass of ice water, setting it before you on a table. The sides drip with the condensation, forming a small puddle around the base of the clear glass. The ice is melting, jostling for position, as you lift it to your lips.

I smile and say, "There's just a tiny bit of poop in the water. Sorry, but it just ended up in there by accident. I hope it's no bother. The rest of the water is quite good, I assure you."

You pause. A tiny bit of poop in the glass; is that enough for you to set the glass down? Don't you want to quench your thirst?

You're not so parched as to compromise on this. No matter how good the water in the glass was, once that minuscule bit of poop entered it, all the contents were spoiled.

That's Common Core, or CCSSI.

Imagine that your child attends an excellent school, where he's taught to do the entire math and reading that any child might learn. So far, fantastic.

The academics are excellent but the moral values are reprehensible: they're also taught to torture puppies. How does one decide? You want your child to learn math, but torturing puppies? Hearing his little reports of how the puppies whimpered in their cages and squealed? Then again, he's surely going to be a good reader...

In life, we must often compromise, but when we apply Common Sense to the hypothetical situation, what *is* a reasonable concession? It seems that pressure to compromise our values is increasing, perhaps because we don't truly consider the consequences.

Trojan Schools

In talking with Ms. Iserbyt I was surprised to hear her concern about the charter school system. She called it the "Trojan Horse" of reform. On paper, charter schools seem great. Parents can take the initiative and get state funding for providing what we would all hope would be an improved school situation. But looking more closely at the charter system, we see the government handing out money to people (the charter's board) who have no standard of accountability. Currently, there's no requirement for elected boards for charter schools. That's called taxation without representation.

Another argument against charter schools is the ability of corporations to purchase them. It happened to an acquaintance of mine, who established a charter school and ran it for several years before selling it. Now a corporation runs that school, and it has ulterior motives, like selling products, and this woman is a convert *against* charter schools.

She argues that this profit-seeking company has skewed the school's operations and agenda, and compromised the integrity or neutrality of education. Teachers must teach to the corporations' demands, and that corporation is accepting school funding (tax dollars) from the government, but is unaccountable to that same government (or the tax-payers). Imagine, for a moment, that Disney controlled all the tablets provided by Common Core/Race to the Top funds. What a great opportunity to instill in this captive audience a desire for new Disney products!

In fact, the burgeoning home school movement, which has grown in leaps and bounds of late (some estimate up to 2.5 percent of school-aged children[56]), is partly fueled by some parents' reluctance to place their children in schools now dominated by product placement. One parent complained about Dora and other licensed characters painted on the hallway walls.

Now, replace Disney or Nickelodeon in this scenario with the federal government. Imagine *their* goals for our children—loyalty, dependency, even blind acceptance. Think about what results would serve those in government and then picture giving them the ability to control what our children learn. Rest assured, *that* is the ultimate goal that the CCSSI strives to accomplish.

The Digital Revolution

Another less immediate goal is to move all education online via devices: the push for technology in the classroom. (And you thought that was a good thing, right?) Although, they've already implemented some of this, they're discovering that children don't always behave like robots and are by no means as easily programmed.

Regardless, the education bureaucracy pushes for tech in the classrooms because digitized education makes it easier for the governments to data mine all of our kids' information, while simultaneously increasing the wedge between parent and child. (No paperwork for little Johnny to bring home from school means even less interaction with parents about schoolwork.) Reducing the need for teachers is an added bonus. No boards, no teachers... Hmmm. This plan is already implemented in Russia, where a wealthy Moscow-born entrepreneur began by supplying schools with tablet computers with which students could learn, do homework, study, and even order lunch from the school cafeteria. It was presented as a good-hearted attempt to bring Russia's education system into the digital era. That was back in 2010.

Fast forward five years and understand that, *"With every keystroke and swipe on his devices, he is building a giant real-time spreadsheet of personal data."*[57] This data is reported to the Ministry of Education. What might the company or the government be able to accomplish with so much free information on each individual, virtually from birth?

In California, the Los Angeles Unified School District board approved $30 million for iPads for 30,000 students, all complete with Common Core apps, at a cost of approximately $1000 per student. Quite an expense per person, for a government ostensibly worried about its failure to balance its budget. If buying in bulk is supposed to save money, who is running this program and where is the oversight? Additionally, due to the rapid rate that these become outdated, costs will increase even more. But apparently, cost is of no issue, when students' data — er, education — is concerned!

Costs

~

"Tell me and I forget. Teach me and I remember.
Involve me and I learn."
~ Benjamin Franklin[58]

The Obama administration's "Race to the Top" funding structure drove many states to adopt the Common Core Curriculum even before it was even written. Here's the salient part of the Department of Education's funding statement:

> *"Adapts the Race to the Top Model of Competition to Transform Lifelong Learning. Widely viewed as leveraging more change than any other competitive education grant program in history, the Race to the Top (RTT) initiative spurred States across the Nation to bring together teachers, school leaders, and policymakers to achieve difficult, yet fundamental improvements to our education system."*[59]

What is that undocumented, unprecedented, and indefinable *change,* or *transformation,* that the administration is so happy about? We still don't know. What we *do* know, is that it's going to be very expensive, and we have specific numbers:[60]

The CCSSI implementation in California will run $2.188 billion, while the federal awards total $104 million. Subtracting the awards from the CCSSI cost leaves a net outlay of about $2.1 billion.

For Illinois, the Common Core implementation is $799 million and the federal awards are $66 million. Illinois will lose $733 million on CCS implementation.

Pennsylvania will experience a $647 million loss; Michigan will see a $569 million loss; and New Jersey will have a $564 million loss on CCS. Many citizens are waking up to the prohibitive price tag associated with Common Core, and they're not happy.

The ultimate price tag on these new standards is in the billions of dollars. "The study by Accountability Works, the Maryland-based nonprofit education advocacy group, estimated that schools nationwide will need $6.87 billion for technology, $5.26 billion for professional development, $2.47 billion for textbooks and $1.24 billion for assessment testing over the first seven years that Common Core is in effect."[61]

There is now an initiative to entirely defund the Department of Education, based mainly on the abject failure and waste that Common Core has proven to be.

As a voting public, we expect to have a say in how our tax dollars are spent, especially when it is such a large part of the budget. Common Core's installation in schools proves to us that our opinions don't count. Even if the price tag weren't worrisome, the treatment of our opinion should. We must wonder what our vote is worth, and Common Core indicates that it has been devalued to almost nothing.

Besides our cold, hard cash, Common Core is costing us our dignity.

EDUCATIONAL FREEDOM

~

"Cuba has an extraordinary resource – a system of education which values every boy and every girl"
~ Valerie Jarret, on Twitter

"What is your position on homeschooling and will it continue?" an audience member at an election rally asked.

Paul Ryan, candidate for vice president, answered:

> *"Absolutely, we have friends who do a lot of homeschooling. In Wisconsin it is very well known, very well used. You know what, we believe in freedom. [Applause] And if you believe the best way to raise your children is to homeschool your children, then God bless you, and in a free society you ought to be able to do just that. [Applause] Absolutely. So yes. Look, we don't want to sit in Washington and micromanage your schools. We don't believe all the best ideas lay in Washington where bureaucrats micromanage. We believe in choice; we believe in competition; we believe in giving parents control over their children's education. Whether that's getting the kid stuck in an inner city school out of a failing school and into a better school, or whether it gives you the ability and right to take over and control your child's education by educating her yourself, that's the kind of freedom we want you to have and preserve in this country."*[62]

Legal changes and challenges

As a home schooling mom, I took a special interest in the 2012 election, because I felt very vulnerable. Freedom to determine how to educate children is fragile in California. This was adequately demonstrated by legislation passed a few years back, which made home education illegal. It's hard to imagine free-floating California viewing home education as dangerous.

Thankfully, an entire coalition of legal and lay people supported the repeal, and it was overturned, providing a reprieve for home educators.

That 2012 election was a referendum on freedom in a broader sense. Having experienced what the law could do, and knowing from history the broad reaches of socialism in the name of fairness, I was more concerned than I'd been before.

For instance, Obamacare infringed tremendously on our personal freedoms—that's what "mandate" means. In San Francisco, taxpayers now fund gender transformation procedures, which are elective operations, (not critical, lifesaving surgery.) Each time we're forced to sacrifice our freedom and resources to fulfill other person's desires, we insult the Constitution and our founding fathers' vision.

Extending this reasoning, if America chooses to gravitate toward socialism, then home education rights are more at risk than ever before. In a socialist society everyone belongs to the state, including, and perhaps most importantly, the children.

Melissa Harris-Perry said it succinctly, "We have to break through our kind of private idea that kids belong to their parents, or kids belong to their families, and recognize that kids belong to whole communities. Once it's everyone's responsibility and not just the household's, then we start making better investments."[63]

Take Scott and Jodi, who had planned a natural birth at home . When their baby came faster than expected, there wasn't time for their midwife to arrive. Scott wasn't at home, so Jodi called an ambulance. Annie was born on the way to the hospital.[64]

The moment they arrived, the staff jumped in to tend to both the baby and the mama. Shortly after, when Jodi started questioning the procedures they were performing on Annie; it became clear the medical personnel were reluctant to answer her. Instead, they called a government social worker, who arrived to investigate allegations, while refusing to divulge what those allegations were. Although they told Jodi that Annie was fine, they said she needed to stay at the hospital for three days, an odd decision regarding a perfectly healthy newborn.

The social worker questioned Annie's care and why Jodi had refused the hepatitis B vaccine. While the social worker came in and out of the room, Jodi wasn't permitted to leave.

Eventually, the social worker informed Jodi that she'd have to sign an agreement for a "safety plan" or lose custody of her child. She said she'd have to wait for Scott who was dropping their other children at a friend's house on his way to the hospital. The social worker said that Scott could review the plan if he got there in time, but if not, Jodi would either sign or lose the baby.

Soon after this, the social worker lost her patience. Jodi hadn't signed the documents and Scott hadn't arrived. When the social worker called the police, they forced her to surrender Annie to a nurse, *without a court order*. Meanwhile, Jodi pleaded with the social worker to allow her to sign the "safety plan" without her husband, only to be told, "That window has closed."

So, having just given birth, she was escorted off the hospital premises, meeting Scott on his way in. They slept in their car, parked across the street, so Jodi could nurse Annie. It was supposed to have been every three hours, but they only allowed it sporadically, and didn't let her stay in the hospital. The following morning, a juvenile-court judge returned Annie to Scott and Jodi, and the case against them was dismissed two weeks later.

Unfortunately, this is not an isolated incident.

In California, Child Protective Services (CPS) arrived with police at the home of a new mother to confiscate her five-month-old son. At the first hospital she'd taken him to for an evaluation, she witnessed a nurse giving him antibiotics, something a doctor had instructed the nurse *not* to do. When the doctor recommended immediate open heart surgery, she and her husband left abruptly without a formal discharge, in order to get a second opinion at a competing hospital.

That hospital concluded that the baby was clinically safe to return home with his parents, but the next day, CPS snatched him away. The parents endured a brutal fight to win back their baby.

Homeschooling Families Can't Teach

These kinds of governmental or at least bureaucratic overreaches and infringements on liberty are too common and getting worse. A recent Canadian case illustrates this.

According to Donna McColl, assistant director of communications under the Education Minister, Christian homeschooling families can continue to impart Biblical teachings on homosexuality in their homes, "as long as it's not part of their academic program of studies and instructional materials. What they want to do about their ideology elsewhere, that's their family business. But a fundamental principle of our society is to respect diversity."

In the incident with the five-month old, the CPS, a part of the government, invaded a home and dictated what was appropriate and acceptable to government, while overriding a parent's wishes. These situations prompt thoughtful citizens to begin questioning.

First, should we respect diversity for diversity's sake? If I believe in teaching hard work and self-motivation, must I also tell my kids to respect laziness? Stealing is wrong. Must I validate people who steal because they differ in opinion, and teach my children to do the same?

This highlights the incredible ignorance of this governmental directive. While the initial path may have been paved with good intentions, the consequences are seldom considered.

Second, should the government tell me what to believe or respect and what I may teach my children to believe or respect? That recent ruling in Canada certainly makes a great case for removing the responsibility of educating of our children from government influence.

You can't serve two masters or two leaders, because divided loyalties lead to collapse. With this ruling, it's painfully clear that the government is bigger and badder, and will win if parents don't push back.

This kind of totalitarianism, a fascism where the government polices its citizen's very thoughts, makes Canada, never billed as the "Land of the Free," dangerous to have as a neighbor.

Here in the US, through their apology, we understand that the IRS was pressuring conservative groups to divulge not only their donor lists, but "the content of their prayers." They have no need to understand Christians' prayers (they never asked for Muslim or Buddhist — or any others' — prayers, but not to worry, those would be next on the list), unless they intend to influence them.

Our rights as home schooling parents are only as strong as the rights we have as free citizens. Sadly, there are those in our country who choose to abdicate choice to the government, allowing it to dictate our everyday lives, despite its proven inefficacy.

Reacting to Ms. McColl's remarks from Canada, Paul Faris of the Home School Legal Defense Association in the United States said, "A government that seeks that sort of control over our personal lives should be feared and opposed."

That pretty much sums up my position on allowing the government to oversee the education of our precious children. It's exactly why I advocate home schooling children.

Consider this report about our Environmental Protection Agency:

> *EPA Administrator Gina McCarthy said that even if the Supreme Court strikes down the agency's pollution regulations, since the regulations have been in place for three years, most plants are already in compliance on Friday's broadcast of HBO's "Real Time."*
>
> *McCarthy predicted that the EPA would win at the Supreme Court. And added "but even if we don't, it was three years ago. Most of them are already in compliance. Investments have been made and will catch up."*[65]

Common Core has taken over our schools. Regardless of how CCSSI may be 'defeated' or 'removed', understanding and applying the quote above assures us the damage has already been done, inside the schools, both with the teaching methods and in the textbooks. Common Core is simply the public education bureaucracy, and until we have a full-fledged overhaul or, dare I suggest it, a dismissal of our public education bureaucracy at the federal level, the best choice is to keep your kids out of any institution aligned with our federal standards.

CLASSROOM PORN

~

"You will ever remember that all the end of study is to make you a good man and a useful citizen."
~ John Adams[66]

The following school material discussion is quite graphic. Here is a transcript of the very first question on a test issued to an eighth-grade Louisiana class:

1. Match the type of sex to the activities associated with it.
a. penis penetrating the vagina
b. penis penetrating the anus
c. mouth and/or tongue on the penis or vulva
Options: anal sex, vaginal sex, oral sex

There are lots of other interesting questions, like where the highest teen pregnancy rates occur, but my favorite is:

Delaying tactics are a permanent solution. (True or False)

Roughly translated, *putting off having sex is not a solution to avoiding sex, because sexual intercourse is inevitable.* Their reasoning? Sex, for teenagers and children as young as grade school, in some cases (in public school), is *a foregone conclusion.* And perhaps they are right, especially when the adults in role-model positions instruct them on the Kama Sutra in the classroom. The same argument may be made for three-year-olds, I should add here. Why put off having sex, at any age, because you're going to do it eventually! It's an absolute disgrace, and it's pervading our public schools. Examine the logic behind this line of thought. All people will die someday; why not just kill them now?

You've heard of hard-core porn and soft-core porn. This is classroom porn.

Unfortunately, this is not a simple one-time event. A Northern California community grew anxious when parents discovered alarming details at Acalanes Union High School District about a Planned Parenthood presentation on campus.[67] When the district finally agreed to identify the people involved in the program, these parents became *more,* not less, concerned. One of the sex education instructors, who worked for a sex toy porn shop called Good Vibrations, located in Berkeley, was known to lead "pleasure workshops," demonstrating the use of sex toys. Although it wasn't clear whether the worker promoted the store's merchandise in school, it was obvious that the association was inappropriate.

Another sex-ed instructor at the high school was a Planned Parenthood education manager for Northern California who called herself a "pleasure activist." Though many of her tweets have since been deleted, she commented enthusiastically about her attendance at the CatalystCon Pornography Conference, which she attended for continuing education credits along with other Planned Parenthood representatives. The event focused on using explicit instructional media for sex education. It also had instruction about the history of sex toys, and tips on *realistically* sharing your own sex life on the stage and on the page.

If you need further convincing of the depravity extant in the public education system, look no further than the Genderbread Person on the following page.[68]

There have been other instances in this same district, of students being coached on asking each other if it's okay to take their clothes off.

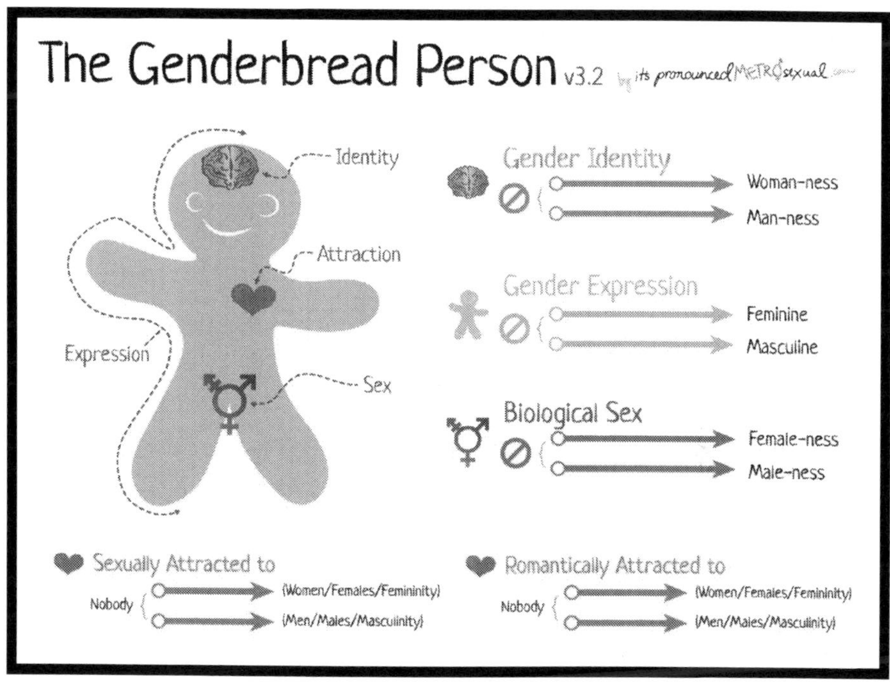

The handout on the next page is intended is to teach comma usage. It was proffered to a sophomore high school English class in Texas, and displayed for the class on the smart board. Personally, I have a problem with public schools wantonly showing children in images of strippers. Perhaps some of you won't disagree with educators placing Stalin in pasties and a G-string, but must they force children to view these images of our president, John F Kennedy? Does equal-opportunity derision and vulgarity make it all right? Absolutely not.

There are other, more effective ways to teach children that do not necessitate vulgarity or overt sexuality, or even sexual innuendo. Parents should demand better of their public schools, or shift to private, where there is more accountability. Ultimately, school at home, where the parent can best monitor exactly what is being taught, would be ideal.

Consider the "Ruby's Hairclip" assignment that teachers originally gave to fourth graders in Arizona. Although the worksheet originated on a teachers' helper website as a learning aid, and was supposedly marked inappropriate for younger grades, it still ended up in the hands of eight-year-olds as an assignment. This text gives rise to serious doubts about the teacher's concern for the children's best interests.

Ruby sat on the bed she shared with her husband holding a hairclip. There was something mysterious and powerful about the cheaply manufactured neon clip that she was fondling suspiciously. She didn't recognize the hairclip. It was too big to be their daughter's, and Ruby was sure that it wasn't hers. She hadn't had friends over in weeks but there was this hairclip, little and green with a few long black hair strands caught in it. Ruby ran her fingers through her own blonde hair. She had just been vacuuming when she noticed this small, bright green object under the bed. Now their life would never be the same. She would wait here until Mike returned home.

Why is Ruby so affected by the hairclip?

How has the hairclip affected Ruby's relationship?

It ought to be considered child abuse to expose children to such adult themes when they are still so young and vulnerable. Often these instances are written off as simple irresponsibility, accidental, but anyone paying attention can perceive a trend. Let's just take a moment to consider how the pornography that is being imposed on our school children can be beneficial to a powerful government. Pornography is highly addictive — equivalent to some of the harshest drugs, in brain chemistry. Addicts are easy to distract and control. Could there be some underlying purpose in prematurely sexualizing our youth, or in convincing them they cannot resist their natural urges, or at least that they shouldn't even try to control themselves?

The following is from the 1963 Congressional Record. These are two of the 45 goals of the Communist plan to take over the United States.

25. Break down cultural standards of morality by promoting pornography and obscenity in books, magazines, motion pictures, radio, and TV.

26. Present homosexuality, degeneracy and promiscuity as "normal, natural, healthy."[69]

If you think that things simply aren't too bad (yet) at your kid's school, you may be right. But consider how long it will be until things cross a line you aren't comfortable with, and how much vulgarity would be acceptable. And also observe that the damage is done *before* you might address it, instead of you preventing it in the first place. It's time to apply Common Sense.

How much poop in your water is okay with you?

Instilling a Lack of Resistance

The ultimate goal of our educators and US educational policy in the 21st century is to train *workers* who do what they're told with *no resistance*. C. S. Lewis said, "If education is beaten by training, civilization dies." Here is Bertrand Russell quoting Johann Gottlieb Fichte, the head of philosophy & psychology at Prussian University in Berlin, who influenced the entire US education movement.

> *"Education should aim at destroying free will so that after pupils are thus schooled they will be incapable throughout the rest of their lives of thinking or acting otherwise than as their school masters would have wished ... When the technique has been perfected, every government that has been in charge of education for more than one generation will be able to control its subjects securely without the need of armies or policemen."*[70]

That chilling quote dates from 1810. Have we come any further in our strenuous efforts in education?

Wikipedia reports, "Any experience that has a formative effect on the way one thinks, feels, or acts may be considered educational."[71] We could extend that broad definition to include playing video games, petting the dog, or drinking alcohol; nonsense, not Common Sense.

Wikipedia's shortcomings reflect our flawed common understanding. We've replaced an emphasis on education with job-preparedness, or *training*. Parents are more concerned with their kids getting good jobs after college, than how or what they learn. This corrupts the classical definition of education, which encourages children to think analytically. But, with teachers constrained like trained monkeys, forced to obey restrictive rules, we can't hope for our children in school to learn to think for themselves.

The mutation of education to Common Core must end if we value our children.

My Common Sense analysis shattered my trust in the government's education system. Until I learned the truth about Common Core, I excused the bureaucracy and it's minions for their educational missteps. I viewed the majority as making acceptable efforts, and knew that there *were* exemplary teachers in the system. Of course, there are exceptions, great teachers and educators, like the beloved principal who brought his school out from the depths.

Wait. Maybe that was a movie. But it was based on a true story, right? The fact that they made a movie about it emphasizes the reality that rescuing a school in the throes of academic death isn't common. It certainly isn't Common Core.

Ayn Rand said that in any compromise between good and evil, evil wins. We face the challenge of deciding how much evil we'll allow before making difficult analyses and finding alternate solutions.

Here are two more of the Communist Goals as recorded in the Congressional Record:

> *16. Use technical decisions of the courts to weaken basic American institutions by claiming their activities violate civil rights.*
>
> *17. Get control of the schools. Use them as transmission belts for socialism and current Communist propaganda.*

> *Soften the curriculum. Get control of teachers' associations. Put the party line in textbooks.*[72]

To reverse the decades-long decline in education and give your children one that will ignite rather than stifle them, there *is* one amazing solution. *It will also challenge and improve you.* It will ensure you know exactly what, how, and how well your children are learning.

Home educate them, or at the very least, assure yourself that the private or Christian school you've chosen does not implement the Common Core or anything that approaches it.

Teaching your children is not nearly as difficult as you might think! (And it is so very rewarding.)

My Story

~

Train up a child in the way he should go,
And when he is old he will not depart from it.
Proverbs 22:6

FIRST THINGS FIRST

~

Our money doesn't read "In Government We Trust."
There is a reason for that.

Why It Can't Be Fixed

Regrettably, public school isn't so broken yet that large numbers of people will notice - not for a while yet. It may not be until this generation has matured into unfulfilling jobs in a failing super-power's struggling economy, without any understanding of fiscal responsibility, that they'll realize the extent of this educational derailment. By then, the damage may be irreparable.

The National Education Association (NEA) was built on irrational sand. Our irresponsible, corrupt, misguided and self-serving government should not owe its citizenry an education. But we are owed value for our tax dollar.

It would be foolish to wring my hands, lamenting, "They didn't teach my son to balance a checkbook in public school," when the government clearly can't balance its own budget. The government's own record of failures has erased my trust in them to provide education for my most precious possession, my children. Heck, I can't even trust them to keep their hands off Social Security.

A healthy dose of personal responsibility pushes me to mobilize my own course of instruction for my kids. Private school, while an interesting choice, is awfully expensive. School vouchers, a controversial subject to many in education, offer some improvement, though they promote charter schools, which are, in short, taxation without representation (no elected school boards). And now Common Core promotes homogeneity. But as I learned watching "The Incredibles," *everyone's special* simply means that no one is. I am inspired to search for exceptional options for the education of my precious children.

In 2008, home schooling was outlawed in California. Happily, citizens swiftly and loudly overturned it that same year. The power behind the teachers—the unions—fear the competition introduced by excellent do-it-yourselfers. This is intriguing to consider, because competition typically *benefits* consumers in other areas of our society. But the public education system and the unions stand against it.

On the bright side, many parents *have* brought school home. They'll show their children how to balance a checkbook and rely on personal achievement, instead of filling their minds with expectations derived from baseless and ultimately unsatisfying theories of equality. When the current governmental spending on these ineffective plans comes to fruition, well-schooled children may, God-willing, find creative solutions for this great country and the vast economic devastation dumped on them. If they don't, perhaps the mis-educated masses will be too stupid to notice or too bored by their own mediocrity to care.

If you've gotten this far in my book, you know what needs to be done. You understand that placing your children in the hands of today's public education bureaucracy is tantamount to throwing them in the lions' den. Unschooling — the kind of home school in which the parent provides very little direction and the student goes through his own discovery — would be preferable! (I'm not a fan of this, just to be clear.)

I get it: being your child's educator is a daunting proposition, but it's not rocket science. I would argue that you are intimidated, mainly because *that's what the education bureaucracy wants you to feel!*

You can home school successfully, educate your kids and cultivate a healthy, loving relationship with them at the same time. You simply need a bit of dedication, love, and creativity. I'll show you how I did it, to ignite your imagination and get you on your way.

So, let's get started.

Permission Slips

~

My family attended a movie premier, a big Hollywood event. Because it was launching a blockbuster children's movie, there were a number of kids in attendance, including mine. For this reason, the premiere started in the early afternoon, and the after-party ended around dinnertime.

My progeny happen to be very polite. (Okay, it isn't by accident - I insist on it, and because they are around me more than anyone else, my way tends to stick.) My husband and I have ingrained in them an understanding that common (or, not-so-common) courtesy is the most basic thing, a way of honoring both God and others, as well as the fastest way to impress people. My kids really like to impress people. They truly make great efforts, and I have conscientiously but gently corrected and guided them at each appropriate opportunity.

As we were waiting for the valet to fetch our cars, another parent turned to me and said, "Your kids are so wonderfully behaved, and so polite!" My children beamed. They love compliments. She turned to her misbehaving, complaining, young kids and said, "Look, we are going home, now, so stop whining all the time, okay? Do you want me to stop for dinner at McDonald's on the way home, okay? Oh! There's mommy's car! Get in the car, okay?" As she walked around to the driver's side, she said to me, "I hope my children are as well-behaved and polite as yours are, when they get a bit older!"

I smiled, nodded and waved. Hope has nothing to do with it.

The fact is, in our culture we almost constantly ask our children's permission for doing things — even when we are doing things for them. "I'm going to make you lunch, okay?" What does 'okay' mean, if not, "Is that acceptable to you?" And, depending on the tone, it might even imply some sort of title, like "Your Graciousness" or, "Your Highness!"

Asking your child's permission, by using the word, 'okay,' is ceding most of your power from the get-go. "Don't pull your sister's hair, okay?" "Eat your dinner, okay?" "I'm going to punish you now, okay?"

It's absurd, but it happens all the time.

Now, think about what happens when the parent sends the child to school. Initially, in preschool or kindergarten, the child is taught that the teacher is the 'expert'. In the higher grades, when homework becomes more challenging, the parent often reinforces that idea. They relegate themselves to nuisances, because they started out behaving as though they had no authority to begin with.

Many parents don't understand authority themselves. I watched a friend reprimand his child repeatedly, in front of me, and the young boy paid absolutely no heed. He finally turned to me and asked, "What would you do, for instance, in this situation?" Now, I concede that my children were angel food cake compared to his mischievous little troublemaker, but that was partly because I established and maintained my authority from the beginning. *Parental authority must be asserted, not assumed!*

I answered my friend, "Well, your first command needed to be obeyed, but there were no consequences for your son, which taught him that you had no authority. It's like the old joke of the English bobby (a cop who carries a baton instead of a gun) shouting, 'Stop, or I'll shout 'stop' again!'"

The renowned security expert Gavin De Becker advises never to answer a stalker. You don't answer right away, because you want them to go away. But assuming that they continue to harass you, you simply don't answer them. You don't answer the fifth time, because responding on their fifth attempt simply teaches the stalker that it takes five times to reach you. My friend had just taught his son that it would take five reprimands before he was actually ready to do something about this misbehavior. For instance, by the time he said, "Do I have to come over there?" it was too late!

There's another side to this, as well. Children must be corrected upon first incident, every time. This is a disciplinary issue both for the child and for the parent. Think for a moment what happens if the parent waits, too tired or lazy to correct a misbehavior at its onset. By the time the parent gets angry or frustrated enough to address the issue, it's too late:

Parent, at wits' end, screams, "Stop doing that! Why don't you listen to me?! I said, cut it out!!"

Child thinks, "Sheesh, what's his problem? He seemed fine with it the first five times — those clearly weren't serious, and now he goes bonkers and gets all angry!"

Or worse. The child only registers the anger coming from the parent. The child sees an irate or furious temper and is frightened of the parent. And it's entirely the fault of the parent.

Braeden is required, as all my kids are, to have his room clean and things tidy before he even asks to go on his video game, which is the reward for accomplishing all his various homework for the day. My rule is that all paraphernalia must be put away, or he loses the privilege of playing. Recently I've even amended this to mean that if he asks before I discover his books awry or bed unmade, he must consequently lose the privilege he hadn't really yet earned anyway — he's lost the right to *earn* the privilege. Who is the one who must be disciplined in this scenario? Braeden? I must insist it is me, more than him! I have to discipline myself to check his work once he asks me, and call him out on misbehavior, and then hold the line in the onslaught of argument that comes after.

In the beginning I was so stringent. He would come to ask, and I would check on his 'status' and find things that needed his attention. Then he would do everything that I demanded, and after double-checking, he'd go on his game. What did I teach him? To come to me for instructions each time, and if I didn't have time to double-check his work, he slid by without getting it done. I don't want to be bothered to provide direction each and every time. In order to make that happen — meaning an easier time for me later — I must insist on good behavior now. And that requires strong discipline — *of the parent.*

It seems easier to be more laissez-faire, but, in fact, the discipline must come up front and through and through, because later, that discipline will be sorely tested and it will certainly fail. When parents send their kids off to school, they often relax the discipline at home. After all, the child is only home for so-many hours a day, etc. Once the discipline is compromised, it becomes much more difficult to regain. Then parents wonder why they have problems, later.

A lot of people believe that home educating would require too much discipline. Their concern is two-fold: they may not be disciplined enough to hold their children to account; and they are afraid their children will lack the discipline necessary to uphold their own end of the bargain.

Wrong on both counts!

In fact, they are missing the point. *Parenting requires discipline — within the parent, and of the child.*

Home schooling *helps* with that.

Institutional (public) school *hinders* it.

You Already Do

~

The Beauty of Home Schooling

In general, no matter what method is pursued, a child's education requires parental involvement. Even if you send your kids to boarding school, there's a minimum of parental interaction, with both the child and the school. Think of homework, or even just the meetings with teachers and principals, fund raisers, etc. The moment your child enters any kind of learning institution, you, as parent, are signed up to also participate on a certain level.

The beauty of home education is that parental investment is self-prescribed. You can easily commit to the bare minimum in the beginning. The secret for success in the process of home schooling is the understanding that it necessarily happens *over a period of time*. This should encourage you to explore the concept, without the impression that you are taking on the weight of the world when you begin. A gradual entry gives parents the opportunity to make mistakes and adjustments, to modify and remain flexible. Remember, the beauty of home education is its *flexibility*, the idea that the program is tailored exactly to both the needs of the child and the expectations of the parent or educator. Any necessary changes come in installments, because as you learn more, your children also morph in their desires and needs.

Similarly, your peace of mind about the perfect neighborhood school can easily change when learning of an unfortunate incident at the school. Or you may realize that your child has an aptitude for science and discover a magnet school for science in the next community. Our culture has made us accustomed to one-stop shopping for groceries and home cleaning products, but when it comes to our kids, more often than not, we need specialty stores. The very best specialist is the parent, because they are the most devoted to the needs of their child. (Of course, there are the scarce outrageous examples of bad parents who exhibit no interest in their children, but for the purposes of this book, I leave them out of the discussion. They won't be reading this, anyway.)

In Your Wildest Dreams

Sometimes the right message takes time to spread, especially if it's going to permeate a complacent, distracted populace. A good message will, however, wait for interest to arise.

I've been an advocate of home education for years, but with the advent of Common Core, the stakes are higher and the debate has intensified, so I eagerly grasp any opportunity to get my message to those who will hear it. A while back, I was invited to speak about home schooling on The Dana Loesch Show for The Blaze TV.[73]

Earlier that same week, right after church, a new acquaintance asked me why I advocate so strongly for home schooling. Because of the noisy crowd I needed to give her a succinct, to-the-point answer. Without too much introspection, I blurted out, "I don't believe an institution is the best place for any child." These words crystallized my passion for children better than I ever had before, and the timing for my epiphany was impeccable.

On Dana's show, I expounded on that analysis. Our entire society has been brainwashed to believe that teacher's have cornered the market on education, that institutional education is the best way to accomplish — what, exactly? *Conformity* and *indoctrination.*

Progressive, liberal, ideological indoctrination masquerades as the government's concern and consideration for our children. The government *doesn't* care, and the sooner we realize this, the better our families will be. This government doesn't care enough about its own bottom line to encourage people to work. Witness the outrageous job-loss concordant with the implementation of Obamacare and the invention of the phrase "job-locked" to excuse it. This alone, should give pause to trusting the education bureaucracy with our precious children.

An acquaintance I met at a social event a few years ago contacted me to talk about her daughter, Jane, who was rebelling against going to junior high school. She'd cry and make excuses to avoid attending and her grades reflected her frustration. A school administrator had suggested that her parents take her out of the system and do a kind of public school home study with her. (This way, the school could retain the child's funds, but be absolved of responsibility.) Unfortunately for the school system, but fortunately for Jane, that program was full, and so, her mom was seeking alternate options.

She began our phone call saying she could never home school her daughter. Although I crumbled inside at her words, I am an eternal optimist. During our chat about the situation, she divulged that when she told Jane to study, she'd say, "I don't *know how* to study!"

That brought to light a real and pervasive problem. They often fail to teach children *how* to study in school. I confided that as a publicly schooled student, it took me until my first year at Duke University to finally learn the best way to study; I gleaned it from a classmate, not from any school instruction, by the way.

I commiserated with the mom that the education system had failed Jane, and I confided that I believed, at that point, the worst choice would be to dump her in another institution.

"But I haven't a clue about how to home school!" she said.

As I expounded on the many options there are to choose from, she finally realized that she wasn't as impotent as our system wanted her to believe. I pursue a classical Christian education for my kids, but there are a plethora of resources for parents new to home schooling.

Her mood brightened. "Wow, I think this might actually be the *best thing* for our relationship. I can take her out of school, cover the basics, and teach her how to enjoy learning again."

I smiled. It had been two years since I had first talked to her about home schooling, but sometimes it takes that long for the message to hit home.

Ultimately, the goal of education is to show children how to teach themselves, to equip them so that they can satisfy their innate love of learning for the rest of their lives. Instead, too often, we see brick and mortar schools instill an aversion to learning from which the youngsters never recover.

The good news is, with access to the internet, great educational materials are mere clicks away, and even the classics are all at the library.

Why Latin?

Tracy Lee Simmons wrote the book *Climbing Parnassus*, as a "defense and vindication of the formative power of Greek and Latin." The author points out that though these languages may be considered dead, they were never mortal. I'm starting to think so, too.

> *Education, that vague and official word for what goes on in our schools, has also been a trinket on the shelves of snake oil salesmen and a plaything for social planners in America for well over a century. They too have been driven by the spirit of ceaseless innovation. And we have paid a high price. The peddlers have shrouded the higher and subtler goals of learning which former generations accepted and promoted. These bringer of the New have traded in the ancient ideal of wisdom for a spurious "adjustment" of mind, settling for fitting us with the most menial of skills needful for the world of the interchangeable part. They've decided we are less, not more, than wiser people have hoped humanity might become. We are masses to be housed and fed, not minds and souls seeking something beyond ourselves. Ask anyone today, for instance, to identify the aims of a "liberal education" and expect a long pause. Everett Dean Martin — he who informed us of our predilection for "new gospels" — wrote a book in 1926 titled* The Meaning of a Liberal Education, and i*n 1973 another scholar produced* The Uses of a Liberal Education. *We might detect in the latter title a falling away from an older ideal. Instead of seeking to discern what a liberal education can bring to us, we now ask what we can get out of it; there's a difference...*

> *The modern mind, schooled to be practical, stands ill prepared to wrestle with these questions because they are at bottom philosophical ones; our practicality has, ironically, rendered us incapable of answering them...*
>
> *We have adopted the leveling assumptions we've inherited* — whatever works for you — *and fed off intellectual capital earned by others who, we presume, have already done the hard thinking for us. We pride ourselves on self-reliance while following uncritically the roadmaps of others. For an independently skeptical people, we ask few questions.* [74]

This expresses so succinctly what I've harped on for so long. It's the main reason for reverting to the classical curriculum, because *not all innovation is progress*. Not all progress is advantageous. These questions remain.: What is the main goal of education? How are our schools answering that question?

I bought yet another Latin book for my oldest to go through for our third year, although we've completed two others. They were both fine for younger children, but as a linguist myself, fluent in five languages, I demanded a solid study book for my oldest, who was then eleven.

Latin has advantages over learning other "more practical" languages. One, it's not nearly as hard as English. Two, it's excellent discipline has been described as training in precise and logical thought. Three, it *is* fun. Latin is a great puzzle, with rules to apply and riddles to solve; it's a game. And, finally, because there's no correct way to pronounce it, it lacks that particular quality that embarrasses a novice into silence.

My oldest now feels capable of deciding his own curriculum. Left to choose, he'd undoubtedly pick plenty of computer game time. T. S. Elliott argued that children were summarily incompetent to discern what they needed to learn.

> *"No one can become really educated without having pursued some study in which he took no interest - for it is part of education to learn to interest ourselves in subjects for which we have no aptitude."*
>
> ~ T. S. Elliott[75]

Surely this must apply to the young, for they're the least capable of determining what might interest them later on. Consider the nutritional choices children make in comparison to their educational preferences. Left on their own, my kids would eat nothing but Doritos and ice cream, but we all know they need appropriate nutrition, just like they need suitable education. I would even argue that some adults ought to learn how to interest themselves in things that seem less appealing to them, like the hands-on education of their own children. Regard it as a challenge — one you can rise to!

I remember my first three-day practicum for a new classical program near me, with an hour each day devoted to Latin. In those three hours, I became fully convinced of how enjoyable learning the ancient language could be. Latin poses an exciting challenge of exhilarating discovery. Learning about one of the main roots of our own language adds tremendous depth to understanding, expression, and comprehension of our literature and culture.

Nothing worth doing was ever easy—but a worthwhile endeavor pays enormous dividends in the end.

The Accidental Home Schooler

~

I first considered home schooling because I didn't want my son to be the youngest in his class. At that time, it was a new concept for me, and entirely terrifying, but having been raised by a strong, self-assured mother to be an education-loving, do-it-yourself-type of person, I decided to try it for his first year of grade school.

Before Braeden entered first grade, I'd checked out the public school he'd attend. We also went to a very exclusive private school and he "interviewed" there as well. Some people think that celebrities get special treatment, and I'd venture to say that while it's often true, it's not always the case.

They turned him down based on his age. Because he was a few weeks too young to join the first graders, they wanted to put him in kindergarten. I was pretty sure he'd be bored out of his little mind. He was finishing at a small Montessori preschool where he had learned the basics of kindergarten and he was ready for first grade work.

The Montessori Method

One quick note about Montessori; Maria Montessori was an Italian doctor who was given charge of the children left behind when their parents went off to work every day. As she researched their behaviors, she discovered that kids like learning.

When given the right tools (i.e., not electronics—at least not *only* electronics), they'd work for about an hour, and then take a break, like an adult takes a morning coffee break. Then, because they had accomplished the lesser task with success, they'd go back to work and tackle a tougher problem, sometimes staying involved for a much longer period.

Her method stressed the importance of giving the children a three-hour work period which permitted success at an easy task and then time to learn a more difficult one. Most importantly, they needed to be self-determined. Some kids don't have a head for math first thing in the day, but can look at and manipulate letters for hours.

Biwa attended a Montessori preschool in Vancouver, Canada, where they implemented very close to the pure Montessori method. Unfortunately, laws for naps and snack time, which impede the self-determination and time-for-work goals at the foundation of the Montessori philosophy, hinder its proper implementation in the US. It is possible that if I had have found a true Montessori school here, I may never have discovered the value in home schooling. I suppose I can thank overbearing governmental regulations for that.

Timing Makes a Difference

Biwa's August birthdate destined him to be either the youngest student in his first grade class or, if we waited a year, one of the oldest in his grade. I hesitated, knowing that the private school wouldn't accept him for first grade that year specifically because of his age. As I considered keeping him home for a year, I discussed it with my husband. He agreed, mainly because with his own September birthday, Kevin had been an older kid in his classes and his school experience was, in a word, dynamite! (Mine was less so, and that's an understatement.)

With my husband's support, I kept Biwa home and taught him a little, to prepare him for first grade the following year. We worked on science, instead of focusing on math and reading, which are the mainstays of education in grammar school. The more informed I became about our educational system, the less I liked it, but I wasn't yet completely convinced on its lack of merit.

We joined a home schooling group that met near us in Los Angeles. Predominately made up of quasi-hippies and seemingly societal outsiders, they deeply valued their children and understood that the system worked against them. They didn't kowtow to the government, instead questioning the authority of a bureaucracy that is a self-admitted failure.

Some of the kids were obviously too smart for school or in other ways eccentric, (we've all met those kids) but they were all very nice. I got along well with the parents, who were mostly atheists. Naively, I had yet to consider the religious aspect of home schooling, so, in searching for a group, religion didn't enter into my criteria (though it does, now). I wasn't, technically, home schooling at that point. I was just taking a year away from the education bureaucracy system.

For this gathering, little of our home schooling was pursued as a group. We simply met on Thursdays in the park, and the kids played while I visited with the parents and exchanged tips and stories. The organizer was a very kind young woman with an over-achieving son named Jake. She recommended *The Well-Trained Mind* by Susan Wise Bauer with the warning, "Don't think you'll do the book justice. It's all just a suggestion because she's like the Martha Stewart of home education."

I read it and I understood her near reluctance to recommend it. But I, too, suggest this tome of information as a starting point to any searching parent, with the same warning.

The ease and freedom during my first year cannot be summarized adequately, except by, "Those were the days." It was a magical time in my family and in life. While Shane, my second son, attended a half-day preschool (play-school, really) in the afternoons, Braeden and I luxuriated in our leisurely mornings and limited stress. Getting off the state school treadmill (before even getting on it) certainly was a gift.

Magic Message

When I was a little girl, working in my grandmother's garden with her, she often had me find and pick off the tomato worms that plagued her plants. It was a favorite pastime and something that kept my clumsy feet and elbows from destroying too much in her garden as well, I suspect.

I loved the cushy, fat green caterpillars with the tiny red horns on their tails. I squealed with delight to feel the small, sticky feet grasp my goose-pimpled skin along my arm, and breathlessly watched them edge their way to find more leaves to devour. To this day, the distinctive smell of tomato plants brings me back to the warm secure feeling of Grandma's hugs, and, no surprise, tomato worms are still a favorite of mine.

So, it was with an overwhelming sense of fond reminiscence that I gazed at three tomato worms in a large jar, which another home school mom brought to the park one day. We often did a kind of spontaneous show-and-tell at our park days. Theresa, a mother of four, shared her new science project with the rest of us. She had a bit of a haughty air, having home schooled for many years already, and spoke tersely in short sentences.

Seeing these companions I'd enjoyed long ago fascinated me. I hadn't thought about tomato worms since childhood, and they raised some long-dormant memories. When I asked Theresa if I could have one, she frowned and said, "No. I'm keeping them so my kids can watch them turn into moths."

What a fabulous idea! I resolved immediately to do the same, but where would I get them? The very next day I went to an appointment in another part of town, and discovered I was right next to a nursery. Perfect. I reasoned that if I bought a tomato plant, the worms were sure to find it. (I had no idea how that worked, but they always turned up in Grandma's garden.) After several weeks of watering and checking the plant, there were no worms. I was losing hope, although I did appreciate how much the little plant had grown. And its tomatoes were delicious.

One day my husband suggested we go to the beach so we headed out with towels, suits, and sunscreen. It was a special treat because, although Los Angeles is on the Pacific Ocean, it was quite a trek from where we lived. I should probably add that I have an aversion to sand; going to the beach was never on my priority list.

When we were packing up to leave the beach, my daughter said she needed to go to the rest room. I hustled her off to the stand-alone building, which sat between the parking lot and the beach, just off the very busy Pacific Coast Highway. There's no shrubbery except a few cacti in planters that intermittently border the sidewalk, which extends the length of the beach, from Marina

Del Ray, past our parking lot and the toilets, on up the coast. The lonely little planter across from the bathrooms was a terse oasis between several lanes of the PCH and parking lot, and the football-field-deep expanse of sand to the ocean.

My discovery still boggles my mind today—there's no logical reason that I should have found this little thing. Walking back from the restroom with Octavia, I glanced down and saw it, booking across the sidewalk from the beach planter to the parking lot. Curious, I bent down and picked up... a tomato worm! How on earth?

The more romantic part of me wants to believe that my grandmother, who passed away before I got married, sent him to me, or maybe God sent him to me, just to show me His love. Holding the silly worm and feeling it moving on my skin, transported me to a time of love and innocence more visceral than the annoying sand on my feet. It reminded me how strong happy memories are.

I showed the kids. I showed Kevin. We brought him home and I put him on the plant, but then transferred him into a large glass jar we used for a makeshift terrarium. We fed him a proper diet of tomato leaves, but he grew sicker and sicker. He started to turn brown and became quite lethargic, eventually writhing in the dirt enough to bury himself.

I was distraught. I didn't know how to help him, and my experiment was in jeopardy. I carried him to the park to consult with the expert, Theresa. I explained his condition to her. "I don't know what's going on. He looked really sickly, all brown and such, and then he buried himself underground."

She put her hand gingerly into the earth to dig him up. To my surprise, she pulled up a brown chrysalis. At one end was a kind of articulated, armored point that thrashed to and fro, as if upset to have been so rudely disturbed. I was as mesmerized as the kids with us. She said, "That's normal. He's fine. Probably be a moth in a few weeks," and unceremoniously reburied him in the soil.

He proved her right, when, a few weeks later, I was standing in the kitchen (where all good science experiments are kept), making lunch. I turned around and to my great delight and surprise, right out of the ground-crawled a great big beautiful brown moth, with wet, drooping wings. Talk about being in the right place at the right time! I had put a stick into the terrarium, just in case, and he used it to climb up so he could stretch out his magnificent, furry wings. He was gorgeous, soft, colored various shades of brown, with circular markings on his wings, and had a fuzzy belly.

He was, in short, a miracle. But sometimes that's how things really work. I took it as a good sign, a sign of faith. I had bought the plant; I had placed the worm in the makeshift terrarium. The rest, the transformation of the worm into the big beautiful moth, might be symbolic of my efforts to home school my kids. If I planted and tended and watered them, would they succeed any less?

By the way, this is the kind of exploration and discovery that a home education environment engenders and encourages. The learning happens all the time, not at requisite hours determined by a bureaucrat, and Mom and Dad learn right alongside the kids, modeling the curiosity and openness to new experiences necessary for a successful life in a constantly changing world.

Unfortunately, at the time, I was too myopic to see this symbolism clearly. Small successes, at least for me, don't afford gross confidence; they give me small confidence. But I am still learning, after all.

Decisions

~

After one year, which didn't actually count because our goal was only maintenance, we moved to an area with a better public school system, just in time to start fresh at a new school. Because I'd basically backed into home schooling without committing to it, public school was still my recognized goal.

Biwa, or Braeden, as he became known in school, had a good year in first grade. The school body embraced him. Popular and out-going, he liked to lead and managed to convince others to follow him. My husband had been popular, so I imagined he was on a social path similar to his dad's; it certainly wasn't mine.

By the end of first grade, even fifth-graders knew his name, and said it with genuine friendship and respect. As for the academics, he performed well and his teacher had nothing but nice things to say about him.

Second Grade Disillusionment

Unfortunately, second grade was close to a disaster. His class had five disruptive students. The teacher-sharing approach meant two teachers alternated days in the classroom. I often volunteered, during which I witnessed several problematic issues arise.

Typically, on my daily run to pick up Braeden, I hung out to chat with the teacher, as I frequently did when I helped with the class. I asked her about her own kids and their activities. When we were together, she'd often brief me about things going on in the school. One day in January, she said, "Today is a very good day." She explained with genuine relief that the five troublesome students had been assigned to special education, which would remove them from her classroom for periods of time. She sighed. I recognized her frustration. I had also experienced the disruptive behavior of these children, as well as hearing one of them swear at another mother-helper in the class.

Weeks before, she'd seated one of the troublesome children next to my son. When I picked Biwa up she'd reported with genuine relief and appreciation that the pairing went very well, that Braeden had helped the other boy with his math for a full half-hour. While I responded with an enthusiastic, "That's great!" my internal thought was an emphatic, "Not his job!"

Then, in February I casually asked her an innocent question that would subsequently change my life. By that time, Biwa had submitted five book reports, one each month, and none had even been returned graded. I was in the room with this teacher who I genuinely liked, helping her tidy up while my kids played in the school yard, and I spontaneously asked, "How are Braeden's book reports? I've never gotten one back."

Without missing a beat, she said, "Oh, not very good; Not good at all, actually."

I was shocked. I'd spent time in the classroom at least once a week, and she'd never told me his work was under par. Because we'd never received grades on any of the five he'd submitted, I had never seen any comments. This came as a complete shock, although in hindsight, I must have asked for a reason. I must have suspected something.

I asked her to show me a "good" book report, and was mortified at the difference between this beautiful, neat, and apparently well-composed paper and what I knew my son's reports were like. I realized that there was work to be done, and was only upset to learn it this late in the year. I could have intervened with him so much earlier, had I known.

I immediately determined to work with him on each future book report. Every day after school, we'd do a chapter in the book and he'd write a summary sentence for the report. The report was actually a hand-out page with lines devoted to each chapter, opening summary and ending summary spaces, and some fill-ins for book details such as title and author.

The excellent example I'd seen appeared to have been done by a little calligraphy artist, judging by the perfect scrolls on each perfect letter. Although there was a great difference between hers and his, at least it gave me a measuring stick.

Each day we labored to compose the few sentences or thoughts that I required of him. We did this at the end of long days when we were both tired, but we got through it. In those moments, I was every bit his teacher. Despite occasional tears, he eventually turned in a much better report, but I still heard nothing from either of his teachers.

After a time, I became quite frustrated with the absence of feedback. However, these experiences piqued my interest in improving the way he was educated. I wondered if there was a better, more practical approach. Having had a taste of the home school experience, I began to toy with that idea and think through its full implementation for my family and me.

The Hawaii Epiphany

Around this time, my husband went off for several weeks to shoot *Soul Surfer* in Hawaii. We planned to visit him on set as a family, because: who turns down a trip to Hawaii? The kids were very excited about our two-week stay and I got fill-in paperwork and homework assignments for Braeden and Shane. Even in kindergarten, Shane had little worksheets to complete, for without them, the school wouldn't be able to collect government funds. And I'm nothing if not a team player.

Hawaii was fantastic. The production had found us a wonderful two-bedroom apartment with a kitchen, on the beach. We settled in easily.

Every morning, we gathered around the dining table to complete math and writing assignments, beginning usually with a little battle about how much to do, and what part needed to be finished. Braeden often said, "My teacher says we don't have to do this in class."

I'd answer, "Well, she gave it to me for you to do, so, here you go!"

I didn't enjoy the power struggle, to say the very least. My son was testing both my authority and, by proxy, his teacher's. That's what children do, though, and understanding that gave me the capacity to persevere with him.

Shane's work was easy for him, though he chafed at doing it before hitting the beach and waves.

The sparkling blue water and white sand shores served as a tremendous motivator. As long as I insisted that they finish the prescribed work, it got done. Then the rest of the day was free to play in the sea and discover the island of Oahu.

While I was working with them in the hotel condo, I realized that I was *home schooling* my kids. Looking back, I recognize the "Thanks, Captain Obvious" quality of my observation, but we often need someone else to make an observation before we can see it ourselves.

A while back, I used to picture myself as unmotivated. Then one day I said it out loud to a friend, who proceeded to laugh uproariously. She pointed out how ludicrous it sounded, by listing many of my accomplishments — all things I viewed as hobbies and not things that could really be counted. It turns out; I'm simply unmotivated in some ways that others *are* motivated. The realization that I *was* educating my kids was a great epiphany — I glimpsed what it might look like if I chose not to send them to school.

I thought about it. You might do the mental comparison that I did. It's one thing to complete some homework sheets in a hotel for a couple of weeks, but another to assume the full responsibility for all the subjects for the year. Most parents help their kids every day after school, but don't realize that they're basically home schooling.

Another concern arose. As I covered the assignments, I lost respect for the material. The worksheets were boring, trivial, and at times, confusing—I wondered why I was forcing them on my kids. I didn't enjoy the presentation, but was obliged to endure it with them, because I was indentured to the system, through the enrollment of my kids in public school.

It's one thing to do a worksheet for twenty minutes, thinking it's not terribly impressive, and retain the illusion that it's not representative of most of the assignments. It's another to continue for two weeks to believe that most of the work that is done in school is somehow more acceptable. It jarred me to comprehend that all the curriculum paled in comparison with what I desired my children learn.

So I analyzed why I had made that choice.

My immediate answer was that home schooling was *hard*.

But, *it wasn't.*

I want to convince you not only that home schooling isn't hard, but that *you've* been specifically chosen to teach your children. (Congratulations!)

Your first reaction may be, "But I didn't sign up for that." We were raised to believe that the government or a private institution would educate them, relieving us of that burden.

Let me assure you that the perception of education as a *burden* is incorrect. It's an honor, a joy, and a privilege! This is why I'm relating our experience, which is leading to a much different outcome than public schools produce.

A Bullying Mindset

In review, I became dissatisfied, first with the service the public school provided, and later with the content, in addition to the social issues that abound in schoolyards today. The bullying on the playgrounds reflects the attitude of the teachers' unions which control those areas by default. Michael Mulgrew, president of New York City's United Federation of Teachers, said this about Common Core at a convention in August 2014.

> *"So I stand here in support [of Common Core] for one simple reason. If someone takes something from me, I'm going to grab it right back out of their cold, twisted, sick hand, and say it is mine. You don't take what is mine. And I'm going to punch you in the face and push you in the dirt."*[76]

He doesn't attempt to persuade on the merits of Common Core with charts and test results exhibiting its efficacy. He can't, because there aren't any. Nor can he use emotional triggers about how the teachers or the kids really like it, for there's no supporting data. He simply owns it, regardless of its negative effects on education, and promises to force its acceptance on the rest of us. No wonder bullying has become a national school issue.

Options Become Opportunities

This is why I believe you, too, will value a *common sense* approach. Like many others, I don't like being forced into anything. I prefer to weigh my options and then make a reasoned and logical decision. It reinforced my satisfaction with home schooling when outrage over Common Core reached a fever pitch.

In any case, I didn't choose to educate at home haphazardly, but took time for a long, well-thought-out decision. I began with a short commitment to test the waters, followed by an evaluation after several months. Even while I researched options and curricula, I hadn't entirely determined to do it. It was late summer before I had a fully formed plan of attack and formally committed to it.

I didn't start with the decision to home school "forever." My experience was gradual, and so, I have long recommended other parents do what I did. Take a small step. I chose to try it for a half-year. That would be enough time to give it a go without losing too much classroom instruction, if afterward I concluded that it wasn't working out.

The System Over the Individual

I wasn't anticipating failure, but the responsibility to educate three children, or even one, is quite heavy. This is mainly because, as I've come to learn over time, we have all been indoctrinated to believe the *system* is better equipped than the *individual.* To keep the pressure that comes with the responsibility light, simply make a short-term commitment. It's okay to say, "If it doesn't work out, there's always the spring semester at the local school, and I can enroll them over Christmas." The truth is, kids can catch up, and school is nothing if not repetitive.

But let me also say here, now that I've been in home schooling for several years, there is no time like the present, and, just jump in! It like the old adage, *You're never really prepared to have children.* You are never truly prepared to home school. All your planning will be undone - and should be, because, well, roll with it - and if it isn't, then you really are the smartest one in the room, so what are you waiting for? Home schooling is a series of trials and errors, as well as overcoming obstacles, but it's also the most fulfilling of adventures.

Let me confess right now—I was *nervous!* I'd gone to public school, attended an excellent university, and acquired a good job and a career. The next steps I had anticipated were getting married and starting a family. My single mother, who lacked a college education, raised me to believe that education was everything.

It actually surprised me when I first realized school might *not* be the best place for my kids. Secondary to that, I was astonished to learn that I didn't *have* to send them to school. But there's a great distance between a realization and an action, especially for an indecisive, insecure individual like me. So I agonized over it. One caveat made it a little easier: *experience.* I had already had the experience of home schooling my children through the travel and after-school homework, and the disappointment of the school not living up to the most reasonable expectations. I became convinced that even if I did a crummy job, I could still improve on the efforts of an uncaring bureaucracy.

Materials and Curricula

After extensive research, I got materials from several different places. Some of the English grammar came from that used by a local private school. I went to the publisher's website and ordered the home edition. History and spelling texts came from advice in one of the "bibles" of home schooling, *The Well Trained Mind*, and other literature that advocates classical education.

The classical method has several appealing features. It aims to prepare a lifelong learner not merely instill a set of ideas or thoughts. The student is encouraged to study the classics and form opinions based on research and thoughtful consideration. It made me wish I'd had more Shakespeare growing up.

Math workbooks, recommended by a friend, came from a major chain bookstore. I recommend involving the children in picking a workbook that appeals to them (while guiding them to your choice). We use an online source that my kids absolutely love for science. One of my guidebooks is edited by E. D. Hirsch Jr. from the series '*What your ___-grader Needs to Know'.* This series provides an overview to make sure I keep up with the public schools, should we decide to reintegrate. It functioned like my training wheels, making balance and direction easy. In the interest of full disclosure, after about a year, I hardly cracked those 'need-to-know' tomes anymore.

In the beginning, reenrolling my kids in public school was always a distinct possibility; not that I expected to fail, but I needed to feel like there was always an out — no decision is permanent. And there are numbers of ways to achieve school at home, including simply subscribing to the online public school and allowing them to dictate your curricula, though I certainly wouldn't recommend that option! Along the way you'll find there are many approaches to developing or purchasing curriculum that works for you and your child.

Note to parents of older children: When you start on a home school journey, be aware that the child's worldview is strongly affected by the school environment. This often leads to a necessary decompression time, once they come back home. Please do not expect perfectly smooth sailing and incredible transformations immediately.

Home education teaches the parent, too - patience.

Innovative Thinking

~

When you embark on this extraordinary journey, first define your reasons and goals for wanting to home educate.

Here's my list:

- We travel. We missed three months of public school over the course of a year due to my husband's work, so I became the *substitute* teacher. I loved the teaching part of that, but the substitute part, not so much.
- Curricula in the public school. I remain unconvinced that the education system is exceptional. (Even bureaucrats and politicians continually talk about how broken it is.) I want *exceptional* for my kids and I can better achieve it with my one-on-one technique.
- Religion. Although this reasoning came to me much later, I finally realized that our education bureaucracy, which teaches only evolution and survival of the fittest, but not creationism or at the very least intelligent design, is completely at odds with my world view. How could I hope to give my children the gift of their religion when everything in public school negates it, seven or eight hours each day, five days each week? Will an hour of some instruction at church be enough to encourage them in their faith? Hardly. Only at home or in private faith-centered schools can we even hope our children will grow in their faith.

Special note about educational standards and ideals: Clinton's former Secretary of Education, Richard Riley, perceptively summed up the need for innovation in our educational system.

"The jobs in the greatest demand in the future don't yet exist and will require workers to use technologies that have not yet been invented to solve problems that we don't yet even know are problems." The best preparation is to create a love of learning that lasts a lifetime. Is that what you got from the public education system? Is that what your children are developing?

Pros and Cons

I intend to train my children to be innovative thinkers. I want them to learn to come up with new ideas that won't be impeded by an instructor with singular focus, limited time and a class of thirty. More importantly, I want my children to develop acceptable habits and norms. Here is a list of the cons that the school environment often engenders.

- *Anti-Family:* Braeden exhibited some anti-family behavior, which may be normal for school kids, but was entirely unacceptable to me. If children normally develop a desire to challenge authority and act independently, then the schools, with their current discipline restrictions and overall culture, seem inadequate to dissuade them or contain them.
- *Bullying behavior:* "A record 209,800 primary and secondary school teachers reported being physically attacked by a student during the 2011-2012 school year, according to new data released Tuesday by the federal government. That was up 34.5 percent from the previous record of 156,000 teachers who were attacked by students in the 2007-2008 school year."[77] It's trending in the wrong direction, and I don't care to gamble that the trend has turned around since 2012.
- *Poor school guidance:* The previous year was disappointing because of the above mentioned concerns and the teachers were less involved than I hoped. My son had to compete with 30 other kids in his class for his teacher's attention, and several of them were specially challenged children. In fact, one day I picked my son up and the teacher told me

she had experimented with seating him next to a problem child, hoping that his calm demeanor might rub off on the disruptive student. It worked, but I was, strangely, not impressed.

- *Wasted time:* Home schooling requires a commitment of three hours a day. I was spending almost that much time just on preparation, commuting and homework. Analyze your overall time commitments: packing lunches, twice daily drop off, commuting with pickup lines, rounding them up when necessary, teacher conferences, bake sales or working on/at the fundraisers, and volunteering in the classroom (both to be useful and as a way of vigilance). All this time is invested on something other than my child—a lot of *not* being with my kids. I didn't enjoy sacrificing time with my kids to spend time with other people's children.
- *Poor curriculum:* The first part of this book is devoted to how our public school curricula are negatively influenced by an educational conglomerate either uninterested in the welfare of our children, or purposefully sabotaging them. The efforts they make, purportedly on behalf of our schools, fall painfully short of being improvements, judging by most criteria. Therefore, I had no confidence they know *what* to teach my kids, much less *how*.

All the above elements indicated I was ripe for home schooling, and needed to select curricula that satisfied my stringent demands.

Is it legal?

Every state has different laws regarding children's education. In California, where we live, the state mandates that every child of school age be enrolled in a school, but it allows me to establish a private school to educate my youngsters, by filing a PSA, or "private school affidavit." I must keep various records, although there's no compulsory testing. Because laws vary from state to state, be sure to get the facts for your particular situation. Home School Legal Defense Association can help with that. They offer insurance for home schoolers, and if you have any legal issue, they are more than capable of shepherding you through it.

What about math?

Quite a few people begin a home schooling conversation with me asking this question. Math is my forté. I love math. I tutored calculus in college.

Perhaps this is why others see me as uniquely qualified to teach my kids.

"Oh, well, then..." the inquisitor answers quietly, nodding.

But wait! That's a misleading question. You don't need to know calculus to teach your child basic math. If you finished high school, and even if you didn't, grade-school math shouldn't be an issue. Be realistic. You cannot agree to let a little addition and multiplication stand in your way. Just because I happen to love math, doesn't mean everyone does. And my preferences wouldn't guarantee my children like the same things, or that they're even good at math. (Horrors!) Rest assured: you don't have to understand non-linear algebra to teach your child subtraction.

So, get over it.

The education system intimidates us into thinking that others are better equipped to educate our young people than we are. Poppycock! Instead, remember that where there's a will, there's a way.

Consider the proliferation of businesses dedicated to teaching your child math, outside the school environment. Why are there so many of these? Perhaps it's because the schools are *failing* to teach even just the basics. On any given day I will walk by one of these establishments to see six-, seven- and eight-year-olds, as well as older children, being tutored in math. If you truly feel inadequate, enlist the support of these franchises — chances are very good you'd end up there eventually, anyway, even if your kids attended public school.

First Steps

~

From the beginning, I involved my children in the conversation.

First, I felt it was important for them to feel like they had some input into their future. They didn't *actually* have much sway over my decision, but they needed to believe they did, because that made them responsible for the outcome. It also mitigated any pushback that might have occurred, if I'd surprised them with this unexpected resolution.

Second, I needed them to be emotionally and mentally prepared, so I planted ideas. When I picked Braeden up from school, I'd say, "If you were home schooled, you would be finished, but because you go to school, now we have homework to do." As a result, they all eagerly anticipated the day they could proudly say that they were home schooled.

My first two weeks as a parent/teacher went off without a hitch, but I'm told that isn't always the case. Not every parent can glide into home schooling gracefully, because so much depends on the reason for keeping your child home. Also, as you'll see, I didn't hold the bar for myself terribly high.

To make life easier, I stuck with the public school calendar and started them on the first day of public school. I didn't have all my curricula in place for the first few days, so we improvised with some material I had left over from the summer. I've regularly had them do review workbooks during the summer in order to keep their minds churning.

For instance, my eldest had horrible handwriting, something never noted by his teachers, so we used free handwriting practice sheets downloaded off the Internet. For math, I took the kids to a large chain bookstore and let them pick out acceptable workbooks.

(I gently guided them to select my choices for them.) Shane, now in first grade, liked his math workbook so well he completed 38 pages by the end of the first week. We encountered a real struggle when he wanted to continue with math instead of switching to the writing assignments from his other workbook.

Although workbooks are readily available, examine the contents, because their efficacy differs greatly. In addition, involving your child in choosing them, makes using them easier.

In the interest of full disclosure, I admit to being somewhat conflicted. If it were up to me, by now my kids would know, well, just about everything. However, I restrained my enthusiasm and over-achievement drive, planned reasonable lessons, and followed the books. I'm happy that we got all that work done, even if my son wrote his book report on Saturday instead of earlier in the week.

Everything Becomes a Teaching Opportunity

My most significant insight gleaned from home educating my children was the actual translation/application of this phrase. It refers to more than simply using dinnertime to teach my kids table manners. It includes taking that time to review the Latin we learned together in the morning. If they were learning Latin or even French, a language I speak, in school, dinnertime would hardly be the place to bring it up; perhaps as a novelty, but not as a matter of course.

Internalizing my ultimate and practical responsibility to teach them has made me aware of how many opportunities I have each day to get the lessons into their brains. We're learning some memorization songs, so we work on them in the car, going to the store. Braeden can sing, in order, all the US presidents. He also likes to prove that to people. To their inevitable amazement I respond, "He's got nothing else sloshing around up there. It's easy for children to memorize and he might as well fill his head with something useful."

In addition, since I'm the teacher, my kids look to me for instruction and explanation *all the time*. Being in charge of teaching them equates to me being the person *in the know*. They don't have to wait to ask the teacher something the next day, which they'd undoubtedly forget. I'm right there. If there's something they want to know, we look it up right away if I don't have a ready answer.

Soon after we began our adventure in home education, as a family, I already could sense a more cohesive, more educational environment everywhere I went with them. That became its' own reward.

Restoration of Esteem

One of the inevitable challenges in sending your kids to any school is that it diminishes your stature in their eyes. You're no longer the authority on things covered in school. The teacher is. For instance, should you be unable to help with a math problem, you drop even farther in their estimation. By allowing public school to teach your children, *you tacitly acknowledge an inability to educate them yourself.* And they surreptitiously understand that. Viewing you as the *secondary* source, they might be inclined to abandon you as an authority on many subjects.

The schools capitalize on this dynamic. Worse, they often encourage it. Don't presume that your relationship with your child who attends public school is the same relationship that you would have if you taught them yourself. It simply isn't. But the entire dynamic changes when you reassert your authority with your child. And it's a better dynamic.

Our third week went fairly well, despite a haphazard attempted mutiny from the troops. I set a solid course beginning at 9 o'clock sharp with Latin. They were to have finished breakfast and be seated at the table, ready to sail.

Incentives That Work

I sound stern, but I broke my own rule even as I laid it down, because there I sat with my tea. Still, I reasoned, students aren't teachers, so I dealt strongly with those not seated, just as Captain von Trapp would have. Okay, not exactly. I told them to do better next time, and then I incentivized them with skittles the next day. Anyone who could name a Latin verb got a skittle. A noun earns another... you see where I'm going with this.

Sugar's delightful appeal to a child worked well for my eldest. Shane, who was only six, could only remember "luna" and "oremus," so that seemed to be a reasonable start. By comparison, he's learning the prayer, the "Sanctus," and Braeden was the one with the workbook. (It was too challenging for Shane with all the writing it required. I wasn't out to demoralize the little guy.)

I launched "Skittles Tuesday," "Jelly Bean Wednesdays," and "Mike and Ike Thursdays." If you are concerned about using sugar as a reward, please remember that I required a great performance for a piece of candy, which is why I chose little ones— and they each earned three, total. So, you dentists out there, calm down!

Braeden had a very well liked first-grade teacher—one of the best. I realized that a major reason the kids loved her was the bowl of candy she kept to reward good behavior. Kids from fifth grade would visit her after school because of that vessel of sweets. My motivation methodology was simply following the pattern of a pro.

On Fridays we had piano lessons. I'd managed to get both boys in at the same time, so it was only a half hour commitment, and then we were off to the public library for our weekly visit. Our local well-computerized library is housed in a modern building without dusty old stacks to rummage around in. This fantastic resource includes a great selection of kids' books and a large, well-stocked salt-water aquarium to distract little ones while Mommy finds something just for her.

We went to karate almost every day when we were in town. Because karate classes were always after school hours, it became my back-up incentive to get the boys to finish their work on time. They responded really well to this motivation and liked the concrete instructions.

I'd purchased a white board for listing school work and chores over the summer, but when the kids started doodling on it, I shifted to computer print outs. In the beginning I started every day with Latin and prayer, but my kids preferred to choose what subject to do when, a hold-over tenet of Montessori, which allows children to do whatever work suits them, for as long as they need. It made sense to me.

For instance, I might need to write a letter to a sick friend, but now isn't the right time. Later in the afternoon, when I'm in the mood, might be better. That's what my modified approach was. Children may know intuitively that they're more open to learning math earlier in the day, but later they want to read history. So, as long as they finished in time to get to karate, I didn't argue. Shane was still going strong with math, and I wasn't about to dissuade him from working ahead. In fact, he was leading me in this.

Relationships

At the end of September of our first year home schooling, I traveled to the Hamptons with Braeden, Shane, Tavia: Igwet, the dog, was also in tow. I got a cheap flight that Kevin was supposed to be on with us, but he landed a movie shooting in Toronto, so I had to go it alone with the kiddies.

We did some work on the plane. I had Shane read a book to me before he was allowed to do math games on his Nintendo, and Braeden had math to do. The only snag in our easy, though lengthy trip, was arriving at midnight at JFK. Taking the train to the car rental with three babies and a small dog in that big city was a bit scary. I felt so vulnerable that I vowed never to book a schedule like that again—I'm a chicken.

The following day we got down to work. Because I had packed the materials, I knew all I had to do was lead the proverbial horse to the water. Now I just had to get them to drink from the fountain of knowledge.

Their main incentive was the expansive beach a short walk from our accommodations. For two weeks, we did school in the morning and in the afternoon I got some of my own work done. Then we went to the beach or spent time with friends. Kevin arrived from Toronto, family members visited, and Kevin and I went into town to meet publishers for his book. Most of my business efforts would have been severely challenged without home school, because I never traveled without the kids. The main reason for this was that I just couldn't leave them. Neither Kevin nor I had family nearby that could look after our young offspring and I didn't feel comfortable hiring someone. Consequently, traveling without my children was simply not an option.

Over the course of those two weeks away from home, a new relationship gradually emerged between my children. In hindsight, it was just them transitioning from the constraints of the institution. Braeden's somewhat overbearing and disdainful behavior toward his younger siblings changed. He became more helpful and considerate, taking on his big brother role with assurance, once removed from the judgmental eyes of his peers and the ageist undertones of the classroom. In return, the younger two grew closer to him. The testy adversarial positions slowly gave way to a more genial sibling rivalry.

Also, because it was my curriculum, I knew each subject (or had the answer given to me in the teacher's copy of the book we were working out of) and understood how it was being taught; I knew what they needed to accomplish and whether they had mastered it. I made games of it when we were just driving in the car. The winner got to pick a treat, or the next game, or the night-time book we read. We had shifted into a full-time home school.

Rebuilding

Before I was a year old, my mother had packed up my sisters and me and moved from our California home. She brought us to her parents in the suburbs outside of New York City and accepted a job in the city, leaving me in the care of my resourceful, loving grandmother for the long days she was working. I looked upon that incredible woman like she was my "first" mother, because my earliest memories are of her. When she picked me up from preschool, she encouraged me, through her open car window, to sing her my new song, even before getting in the car. She called me "Dearie." We would take walks together around the reservoir before getting ice cream at the new neighborhood place that had just opened.

I was devoted to her, so it was difficult for me when, in second grade, my mother remarried and we moved away from Grandma and Grandpa to live in a new house with my stepfather. I realize now that I suffered great depression from this change, though at the time, I probably hid it pretty well. One day my mother found me crying in my room and asked me what was wrong. I shook my head, not even knowing how to answer her. She guessed at a few things before hitting upon my grandparents. The moment she mentioned them I started a new round of sobbing.

"Are you afraid Grandma and Grandpa are going to die?"

I nodded, suspecting that might be why I was so sad. I think now it was simply the profound sense of loss hovering over me.

So, we called my grandmother, with whom my mother had a distant, frigid relationship, to calm my fears and reconnect me. I felt better. Hearing her voice was always a great panacea.

She laughed into the receiver. "Oh, Dearie, I don't think I'm going anywhere anytime soon. I may be old, but I've still got a lot of kick in me."

That was an understatement. The spry woman wasn't afraid to tackle bee hives, suffering countless beestings with a shrug. At at the age of 69, she had leaned a tall ladder against a tall tree in an effort to tie a rope for a dog run. Having watched her climb up about eight feet, I asked her, "Why don't you open up the base of the ladder. Wouldn't that be safer?" She answered that it wasn't necessary, but I saw all the pine needles at the base of the old tree.

She went over a wall as she fell — the ladder slipped — hitting the ground four feet below the ladder's base, and I had watched, helpless. Her leg shattered, she said, "It doesn't look like I can get up from here." The ladder lay across her sprawled body, compounding her injuries. "Why don't you run and get me some help, please."

I did. The doctors said she wouldn't walk again. They were wrong, of course. They couldn't fathom her tenacity and drive. She wouldn't even stay down for long. She insisted on a walking cast, and healed fully enough that you wouldn't know she had ever shattered her leg. Her unwillingness to concede defeat was infectious. I like to think I got some of that from her.

Once my grandmother moved to the west coast, my visits entailed lengthy summer stays at their retirement village. They were never long enough. We would tend her fabulous garden together (I would still search for those infuriating tomato worms!)

We enjoyed taking long walks to gather blackberries. We made jellies and jams, and walked the Spit, a sandy beach that jutted out into the ocean. My grandfather also enjoyed my visits. He taught me to play bridge and cribbage.

As I approached adulthood, I didn't have time to visit anymore. I had to work all summer to pay for college, for one thing. Then I started traveling the world in my modeling career. Overseas phone calls were expensive, especially from hotel rooms; I kind of lost touch with Grandma.

I remember trying to reestablish my relationship with Grandma once I settled down in New York. I started calling her each Sunday. Initially, she was reluctant to talk, thinking, perhaps, I was making a hollow gesture.

"Oh, Dearie, now, you don't own stock in AT&T and this must be costing you a fortune," she'd say after a two-minute conversation.

Grandpa had died when I was in college, and I can only imagine the loneliness she felt. It took several weekly sessions, me prodding her with questions just to keep her on the phone, before she began confiding in me about her doings and feelings. That's the stuff of real relationship: the bridge partners who gave their hands away, her triumphs with the roses and tomatoes, or sorrow over her friend's illness. Eventually, we augmented the weekly calls with yearly visits. I miss her today, and I'm so thankful I had the foresight to invest in a renewed connection.

Kids are much more open to revamping relationships than eighty-five-year-old grandmas, although they still must be taught how to manage one. I needed to work with mine on their relationships with their siblings, as well as how they dealt with their father and me. Part of this need is completely natural - after all, they've never done 'life' before. Part of it, for my older boy, certainly, was because the school environment had exposed him to things that were harmful to our familial connection. School encourages an independence that can easily become disdain and disrespect in the continuing absence of the parent, and to a small degree it had for Braeden. In addition, it was important for me to understand the transition time that was necessary for Braeden.

Today's culture, and the push for education, asserts that the school faculty is the fountain of knowledge, and the institution is the only place to access it. How radical, then, to recognize that as parent you are your child's initial and enduring source of wisdom, instead of some government bureaucracy! In fact, as you continue on your home school journey, your family will eventually discover that knowledge is available nearly anywhere in the world, at any time. "Educators" don't 'own the territory.' A greater discovery is that sometimes you, as parent-teacher, are learning alongside your child, modeling for them how to obtain the wisdom they seek and practice discernment with the bevy of information available.

My kids' understandable hesitation to do school at home met my velvet-gloved, iron-fisted determination to overcome it. My authentic enthusiasm over their smallest improvements eclipsed any reluctance on their part. I actively and strategically sought out opportunities to foster closer relationships between all of us, during both playtime and work time. The home school environment recalibrated our parent-child relationship.

Those earlier efforts with my grandmother had been building on a solid foundation, created years before when I was a little girl growing into adulthood. Later, I had only to unearth the base and start reparations on the old edifice.

While it's almost as simple with children, it is the foundation that needs reinforcement and perhaps expansion, to begin with. It's hard work fortifying an early trust that was rejected or transferred to the school institution, but it absolutely can be done. I've seen it.

My younger ones adapted quite easily to our new systems and practices. My eldest child understandably required more time to 'settle in.' For older offspring, especially those having attended preschool, making the transition from public school to parent school is a major shift in worldview, and while school at home provides the platform on which to build strong family bonds, those still necessitate mindful, quotidian investment. In other words, a weekly phone call is entirely insufficient. It requires patience before the student grasps the new paradigm, especially if he is accustomed to public school and being away from home for long periods of time. Don't allow insignificant issues to become too big and don't pick the wrong hills to fight for, but do insist on the minimums, while cultivating your desired relationship with your child.

I crave intimate, enduring relationships with my children that will withstand cultural and societal assaults. I refuse to be relegated to the sidelines, observing their lives unfolding farther and farther away from me.

By the time we returned from our trip to the east coast, I realized that this essential, most desirable construction project had begun.

WEEK SIX

~

Week six of home school was great for a few reasons. First, Shane's *Shurley Grammar 1* moved him from the more banal 'learning-to-classify-stuff,' to actual English grammar, which begins the labeling and categorizing of English words. This is kind of like decoding to a young boy. In other words, virtually irresistible. Also, we finally started to settle into a schooling rhythm. Lastly, I like to be back home after any trip.

The first reason for this week being a success is the most interesting. *Shurley Grammar* teaches children English grammar and writing. It reveals to growing minds how language is organized, with classifications and jobs for all the words, and even the purpose for each sentence, in any piece of writing. Do you remember how to define a subject or a dangling participle? Although I excelled in grammar during my school years, I can't remember now. But I'm saved by *Shurley*. Surely, *Shurley* will teach me!

During our first weeks of home school, Shane and I spent all of our grammar time cutting out pictures of things in magazines and sorting them into categories in various ways. *Shurley Grammar* instructed us to paste them, pile them, and put them in folders. This week, for the first time, we read sentences and determined the subject noun and verb in each sentence.

Shurley has handy little jingles. The first one, sung to the tune of "This Old Man" helps kids remember what a noun is. "This little noun, floating around..." defines a noun as a person, place, or thing. After reviewing the jingle, we began with parsing our first sentence. To do this, there are standard questions to ask.

It sounded like this:

"Dog runs."

"What runs?"

"Dog. Subject noun."

At this point, Shane labeled "Dog" with SN, for subject noun.

"What is being said about dog?"

"Dog *runs*. Verb!"

Next, we labeled the verb "runs" with a V. I didn't realize how much fun Shane thought elementary grammar was until the next day. Daddy was going to run an errand and asked if the boys wanted to come with him. (I'm fine with that, as long as they understand that homework is still due. And they love to goof off, or do anything, with Daddy.) Shane, standing next to me in my office, said, "Mommy, I don't want to go with Daddy. Can we do some more of that 'SN-V stuff, like yesterday?"

Where had that come from?

I was astounded. "You bet we can." So, for the next four days, we did not only the three sentences in the book, Shane insisted I come up with extra ones for him on the fly. ("Braeden farts," got a big response. "Braeden: subject noun. Farts: verb.")

The intrinsic value in this method is that once students appreciate and learn the organization of language, they can apply that approach elsewhere, making it easier for them to get familiar with and comprehend other subjects. I didn't care if Shane, like me, didn't know what a dangling participle was when he was thirty, but his mind needed to understand that language, learning, and life, all have an underlying organization. Learning this structure gave him the experience of how to break down and comprehend bigger and more complicated things.

Some people never learn to do this, to their own detriment. A person may argue a point and hear it soundly refuted, only to return to the same line of reasoning a moment later. This is because the individual can't organize the simple elements of the argument into proper classifications, like "invalid."

Braeden was also doing the *Shurley Grammar* curriculum, two years more advanced than Shane. His third grade book laid out more intricate lessons. It included nicely worded teaching scripts for reading directly to students, whether one or many. It had five lessons per unit, which equated to one unit per week. That structure kept me from missing a day, because, having an appreciation for order, I wanted Monday to always be day one of the unit.

Four days a week Braeden learned parts of speech and usage. Thursdays were test days for Braeden. Fridays were for writing practice, meaning expository paragraphs that were taught sentence-by-sentence. I remembered with mild disgust the template Braeden had for book reports in school, with questions to describe not so much the plot, but just the things that happened in each chapter, as if each chapter were independent of the others. That simplistic method led him to simply copy the first and the last sentence of each chapter directly out of the book as his summary of events.

Now, I no longer spent my time reviewing the book with him and trying to teach him how to word the summary to encompass the events in the chapter. Instead, I taught him the three-point paragraph, a fundamental building block for mounting a persuasive argument. This is a structural tool he can use for the rest of his life.

And, at the same time, *Shurley* may actually have improved my writing, or at least my dangling participles.

A Low Profile with Outsiders

Our karate studio happened to be less than two miles from our house, and offered us a flexible schedule we could work with, between out-of-town trips. One reason I chose to home school was because we frequently travel. Another reason we loved this facility was the head instructor and owner, Johnny, believed in praising the kids for good work, but correcting them definitively when they were wrong. I remarked more than once on his subtle humor when he was teaching, much of it directed at the parents who were observing.

Both Braeden and Shane began as white belts. On a breezy southern California Wednesday, the teacher asked the students how they were performing in school. Braeden answered, "Good. But I don't..." Then, out of embarrassment, it seemed, he stopped talking.

Johnny said, "Well, Braeden, at least you're honest," laughing with the other parents, who also thought it was funny.

What they didn't realize was that Braeden had simply avoided saying that he was home-schooled. After we began home schooling, I'd needed to warn the kids that it wasn't appropriate to just blurt it out to strangers, because, as talkative as they were, they were apt to tell everyone they met. I do mean *everyone* - whether or not they'd even started a conversation. For instance, Shane might approach someone in Michael's and say, "I'm in the first grade, but I don't go to school. I'm home-schooled, like my brother. He's nine."

I knew I needed to put a stop to that. Ventura County, where we live, is quite receptive to home schooling, but Los Angeles County, not so much, and we live right on the border of LA. For this reason, I often do my errands with the kids in the afternoon, when others easily assume they've been released from school. It might not be so evident with one child, but three makes it more difficult to fly under the radar.

We're noticeable. For many, my concern may seem odd, but there are people who report truancy, which is a crime of the parent, who is responsible to get their children aged six and older to school. Home schooled kids aren't truant, but I don't need the aggravation or attention of an investigation.

Since our schooling time falls between nine and usually one- or two-thirty, afternoon errands are logical. For this reason, it's seldom necessary to discuss our education situation with others. It shouldn't even come up, except for my motor mouth kids and my inability to control my own excitement about it. Still, that's reserved for specific, reasonable occasions, not strangers in a crafts store.

Reveille Academy

One day I sat the kids down and said I needed their attention on an important matter. "Now, I don't want you to lie. But I also don't want you to blab. Some people are less receptive to the idea of home schooling, so from now on, you will simply tell the truth, which is that you are enrolled in a private school. Can you say that? Say it: I go to a private school." They did.

"What if they ask us the name of our school, Mommy?" Braeden asked.

"Then you can answer them, 'Reveille Academy.'" I pronounced the French word with a French accent: 'rev-ay.' "That's the name of our school."

"That's a crappy name. I don't like it." Braeden has a quick, critical mind, to put it nicely. "Let's call it Buttfart Academy. That has a better ring to it."

Oh the joy of these little, unencumbered minds. Shane burst into laughter, and Tavia's giggles were contagious.

After I calmed down, I said, "Well, I'm sorry you feel that way. If you'd prefer, you can pronounce it 'rev-uh-lay' Academy. But that's the name of our school." I was so matter-of-fact, I invited no argument.

It worked. Braeden said, "Oh. Okay, I like the first way better. Reveille. Shane, can you say *reveille*?" He loves being the big, knowledgeable, older brother.

They all said "Reveille."

Then I explained to them that the name means, "to awaken," but is a homonym for "to dream." My sister, their aunt, suggested the name. The French word "reveille" gave us not only the name for the military morning trumpet call, it is also distantly related to reveal, which is particularly meaningful for a school. So many games to play with this word; I love it!

Now that my kids know the name of their school — it hadn't occurred to me to tell them before — they seem to feel more invested in it. While they still aren't overly shy about announcing that they're home-schooled, at least now they have a subtle understanding about privacy, for themselves and our family, and they're more careful to protect it.

That's a revelation.

We Don't Need No Institution

~

After instructing my children for a year, I received a group text from a friend encouraging a number of us to gather at a local eatery after drop-off the first day of public school.

> *Join us for the 3rd annual "1st day of school mourning" (I mean morning) after drop off...*

One woman responded she would be there after swimming from her puddle of tears, and another asked if it was necessary to be in mourning. A lot of jokes were made, and I laughed, too, but in a more melancholy tone.

The Home School Perspective

My anxiety about getting my kids back in school was from a completely different perspective than theirs. I looked forward to time at our kitchen table, learning geography and history together. I wanted an excuse to be involved with them, instead of concentrating on my writing. I anticipated getting them to ask questions, making headway in various subjects, and seeing their excitement about learning.

Don't get me wrong. We don't have an idyllic Norman Rockwell existence, as my boys and their infamous (read "deadly") farts will attest. (Those emissions often interrupt the most important point of the history lesson, too, and are followed by uproarious laughter.) But in spite of the frequent, necessary evacuation drills, we usually get through our day. School is like eating an elephant — one bite at a time.

I love our organized chaos, the schedule we cannot, no matter how hard we try, adhere to, and the fact we still get our studies done, through my cajoling and threats of no more TV ever, or extra math pages. It isn't all rainbows and unicorns, but I enjoy the dogged, pragmatic, plodding that goes with the territory. And the rewards can't be beat.

Independent

My first son, Braeden, mulled over changing his name. He was considering reverting to his old nickname, Biwa, his self-appointed toddler nickname, which he developed when he was learning to talk. He asked me if he should change his name, worried that the other kids might make fun of him. I explained to him that kids will always find something to pick on, whether you give it to them or not. They wouldn't need a strange name if they wanted to tease him. They'd find something about him, his clothes, his hair, his teeth. Kids find the oddest 'reasons' to pick on other kids. I'm a firm believer in the strong-name-creates-strength view.

I also told my amazing child that his name defined him only if he let it, and only how he wanted it to. I never saw a problem with *Biwa* when he first hit upon it, but eventually he realized that it's an odd name. He would often get a questioning look when he introduced himself to people as "Bee - wah."

Who am I kidding? He received a screwed up face and a, "What?" Still, he liked its distinction. He began leaning in to new acquaintances, like he was imparting a secret, when he introduced himself. That had an amazing effect on people. I know - I saw it.

Biwa is a name unique to him (so far) and that appeals to my go-getter son. So he chose to revert to this strange, entirely untraditional, made-up name, which happens also to be the name of a Japanese stringed instrument.

After retraining myself to call him only Braeden (I had used his nickname for a long time when he first claimed it as a toddler), I struggled to remember to use Biwa, so I often resorted to Sweetie, but I think he was on to me.

Back to School?

A commercial shows at the same time every year:

♪♫ *"It's the most wonderful time of the year!"* ♫♪

It's not for Christmas, but a Back-to-School ad for a major retailer. It shows parents skipping and dancing down the aisles, loading their carts with school gear. I laughed when I saw it, but as a home schooling mom, I speak for many like me when I remark, "How sad."

It's lamentable that parents are happy to send their young children off for seven or eight hours each day, not really clear about what they do or with whom. Afterward, they may help with homework, but not in the real essence of the subjects, because they didn't choose the material. They check off boxes on a chart where someone else decided what was important for a child to learn.

I never knew I was such a rebel until I began home schooling. I don't want my child to dance to someone else's tune. I want them to compose their own. And I want to help them discover it.

Getting the "Good" Teacher

"What do you think of your daughter's first grade teacher?" I asked my friend.

Some teachers develop reputations they can't avoid. Students love some, but consider others harsh or without personality. To avoid a stampede of parents trying to have their children placed with the "good" teachers, some schools have enacted strict policies removing the parents from the process. Assignments are posted one day before school begins, and no one is allowed to ask for changes, until they have verifiable grievances *after* classes start.

She shrugged. "She's supposed to be good, but I guess I'll find out."

How frightening to send your child into a class with a teacher you know nothing about, trusting the system to deliver someone capable, inspiring, and compassionate. In time, she *will* find out, and I hope it *is* good news.

We have a little friend who has two teachers. When I asked her how she liked them, she said she liked them both, but sometimes one of them was mean. What that might imply is anyone's guess.

Another friend has twins who in three years had never been assigned different classrooms. However, with no explanation, this year the principal made a blanket ruling to separate all twins. Luckily, my friend didn't have an issue with that, because she and her husband had been considering it, and this turned out to be just the impetus they needed.

I still wondered, when is making a blanket resolution in the best interests of the individual children? Perhaps some parents, who know their children better than school administrators, wouldn't want their children separated; Quite a change from the days of "Father Knows Best."

Because we grew up with institutionalized education, we assume it's the best option, the only option. Home schooling, unheard of when many of us were in school, offers a different choice. It raises questions about whether the institutionalization of anything to do with our individual children is really in their best interests.

Public Speaking

Ten-year-old Biwa gave his first public speech. He chose the topic: sunglasses. He explained the different types of sunglasses and their various purposes and costs, and he even used props, going so far as to break a pair for the audience as proof of their fragility!

Classical Conversations was an organization I was investigating for my home school endeavors, and they produced this three day *practicum*, including the public speaking portion for children. Biwa specifically asked to deliver his speech to the largest audience possible at this event, so I told him he would have to arrange it through his tutor there. I was kind of embarrassed to push him forward as he asked me to. His persuasive charm prevailed, and he gave the speech for the entire group of parents.

I helped Biwa write it, but the laughs he got were all his, as well as the applause, except for a few parents who clapped me on the back. I got to experience his success in a much more profound way because I shared so intimately in its development.

Per Diem

~

A typical day…

Each home schooling family develops its own patterns and schedules. This book is intended to give you a window into our journey. The following was a typical day our first year.

I usually get up at 5:30, with no alarm. While I'm devoted to a book project, the prospect of writing wakes me up. I sit with a cup of tea and type at the computer for about two and a half hours. At eight, I do a quick email run-down and then head upstairs to change out of my bathrobe and get ready for the day.

The kids usually wake up between six and eight, the little ones sometimes not till 8:30. They get to bed later when Daddy's home than when he's not. Today, Braeden is up at 7:30 and he's allowed to watch cartoons until 8 after which there's no more television. That's sometimes enough incentive to get him up early. By eight twenty, he's eating breakfast and the other two have wandered down to the kitchen. Kevin is Breakfast Man, so he's helping them with eggs and cereal while I get dressed.

I like to start the day with them at nine. We begin with a short review of some Latin words at the kitchen table. Today isn't the lesson day, just a review, which goes quickly, and we're off to other subjects. Biwa wanders into my office to do spelling, with headphones and a study DVD. Our spelling curriculum is called The Phonetic Zoo. It is an independent, self-driven spelling course that teaches a new spelling rule with each new lesson. He takes one fifteen-word spelling quiz every day, advancing to the next test only after completing the current test twice, two days in a row, without mistakes. There is no real study involved, but I assign him writing the missed words three times correctly.

Shane and I get started with his "SN-V stuff," (subject noun – verb,) or *Shurley Grammar,* as it's more widely known. He loves it, although it is hard to get him committed, when in his estimation, there are so many other more interesting things to do. Once he's seated, he's thrilled to be able to identify all the words and their jobs in the three daily sentences, as well as learning his new vocabulary. We complete a lesson about writing a two-point expository paragraph and he's surprisingly eager to start it: My Favorite Colors. In just under 45 minutes, we're done.

I turn his math book to the next two pages for him to complete, sending him off with a kiss on the cheek.

I call Tavia for her daily reading, but just as I do, the phone rings, and I have to take it.

Afterward I wrangle her and we sit for a little bit of reading. She's just getting her letter sounds down, so it's quite a struggle, but even she can appreciate the progress she's making. After about ten minutes, she complains about being too hot. Her attention is shot. I gently insist on finishing the page, which we get through with my extra help, and then she asks sweetly, "Mommy, can I take a break now?" Of course.

Biwa finds me still at the kitchen table. "Mom, it's time to do grammar."

Although I have to take care of something with my assistant in the office, I'm back in less than ten minutes. When I return, he's at the table imagining some battle between his Lego warriors. He says, "Okay. Let's get started, please."

Today's lesson is on quotation marks, so after the daily sentence parsing, I read through the lesson with him, go over the practice section so he knows what to do, and set him free.

Now I have a chance to catch up on the emails I've been ignoring, but not for long, because Shane is having trouble with the last page of math problems. That takes no time at all to sort out—he was stuck on the name Tonya in the word problems. He finishes that page as I dig out his reading book in which he has two pages of reading lessons. While he starts that, Biwa practices the piano. Shane sneaks over to the piano when reading is finished, and Biwa comes back for history about Christopher Columbus. I read aloud to him, plus he has two chapters to cover in his book about the explorer.

I call out to Shane and Tavia, "What do you want for lunch?" while Biwa finishes the history lesson by himself.

Usually, we eat lunch at the TV while watching educational videos from the library. Today, instead I tune into the History Channel's program on Alexander the Great. Biwa and I are fascinated with this iconic historical figure, but the little ones lose interest as soon as they finish eating and head outside to find grasshoppers and snakes.

Biwa finishes up his Bible work and math after lunch. He still has reading to complete, but I send him outside to shoot hoops for a while.

Afternoon Activities

In the afternoon, we have two karate classes. Biwa has recently advanced into the orange belt group, so the boys are no longer in the same class, but because Biwa finished his work before 1:30, he gets to play phone games at karate while Shane takes his class. Tavia has a play date there with her BFF, the younger sister of one of Shane's classmates.

When we get home, it's time for chores. Shane unloads the dishwasher while Tavia helps with forks and spoons. He corrected his grandmother the other day for calling it "cutlery." It was funny. He had never heard that word before! Biwa loads the dishes while I make dinner. He's learned well, and does it perfectly, making me so proud (and grateful.)

After dinner today we decide to play mancala, a strategy game with marbles, on the new iPad. I love it although Biwa thrashes me soundly. Then we do a round of Shoots and Ladders, so Tavia can join in. Soon, it's off to bed for all of us. I'm exhausted, but happy.

Time Recaptured

From the above description you can see how busy life is with three home schooled children. Although it sounds tiring, here are things I've eliminated from my schedule by not sending them away to the local public school every day:

- Making daily lunches
- Rounding children up to take them to school each morning
- Driving to school each day
- Rushing around looking for lost books or papers
- Reading/signing forms sent home from teachers
- Planning school parties / baking things for school parties / shopping for school parties
- Doing homework at 4 p.m. right before dinner
- Doing homework after dinner
- Feeling stupid because of not understanding the 'new' math
- Driving back to school / Waiting in pick-up lines for kids
- Parent-teacher meetings
- Dealing with bullying or handling playground incidents (after the fact)

Despite our relaxed situation, kids need to put on shoes at some point during the day, but many of these elements are handled without the added stress of marching to someone else's drum.

I still have to do homework with them, but without the stress. Bullies are still out there, but I'm usually right there to run interference, before issues get out of hand or distorted.

And parent-teacher meetings take place in my mirror.

PROBABILITY

~

QUESTION: What's the probability that Biwa will complete all of his schoolwork before 1:30 in the afternoon?

ANSWER: Very high. A half-hour of video games for doing so is too great an incentive to resist.

Incentives

It took several weeks before I established an assignment schedule with the right format for Biwa and Shane. It wasn't fancy, but simply listed day-by-day the week's work in various disciplines, as well as extracurricular activities like karate and piano. Biwa liked to cross off each subject when he'd completed it. He ignored the little check boxes to the left of each subject, but instead scribbled through each name on the list as he finished them. He was further motivated by afternoon classes like karate and basketball, which were his rewards at the end of his days. Being late for karate meant that Sensai wouldn't let you in. I placed the power in their hands—an important step in fostering independence and self-reliance.

Shane, being younger, struggled with this approach, so I decided to be more hands on with him, but it worked with Biwa. He began to set an alarm and get up early, to start his spelling at just after eight, and finish all of his work by 11:15.

Strangely, his commitment presented me with an interesting conundrum. My delight in his progress was accompanied by doubts about myself as a teacher. He demonstrated consistent enthusiasm to get right to his work, attack it, and complete it. Obviously, he enjoyed the sense of accomplishment and control. Funny thing, though, Biwa was a consummate procrastinator.

Anything that would instill the better choice of timely attention to projects was certainly what he needed, so I was happy to see it working. The more often he finished early, the easier it would become for him to apply this principle to the rest of his life.

But my self-doubt continued, making me nervous. Was I giving him too little work? Was he doing a good enough job? Should I just send him to public school and let the teachers agonize over whether he was being well educated or not?

The answer to the first two questions was easy enough; no and yes. He was learning. I checked his papers at least every other day, to make sure that he was doing them properly and not rushing through his work sloppily. I could always give him more, but we were easing into this new paradigm, and I didn't want to overwhelm him. I slowly added a little more. In the meantime, I was content because he was performing well and improving.

As for the third question, I had to keep reminding myself that there was no guarantee that a public school teacher would be as concerned as I was in my son's education. Had I forgotten how his second-grade teacher failed to notify me his book reports weren't good? Had I so quickly forgotten how non-educational that work was - that even the book reports were more like busy-work?

We often hear how overtaxed and resource-limited teachers are. After experiencing good, mediocre, and bad teachers, I've decided not to spend my time helping them or fighting with them, or even volunteering at the bake sale. I prefer to spend my time making absolutely certain that my children receive an education we can be proud of, with my full commitment.

However, that reasoning failed to placate my fears of inadequacy. What calmed my anxiety was seeing my children blossom, watching their growth in language and writing, and experiencing improved relationships with them. I also enjoyed other people's positive comments about their behavior and attitude. My friends had noticed their improvement, too.

Manners

As I grew in my teaching role, I understood the depth and breadth of my responsibility. Eventually, I insisted my children employ "ma'am" and "sir." "Why?" you ask. I admit that may sound extreme. After all, I don't live in the South. Here's the reasoning. "Please" and "thank you" are so easily forgotten that I figured the kids needed an additional incentive to make the politeness rule stick. I figured that if it became more of an issue, there was a better chance they'd remember. It worked.

Now, I simply wait an extra beat before answering their requests, until I get a quick "Please, Ma'am?" with a smile tacked onto the end. Better than that, when we're out, and they speak politely, other people look at me, and raise their eyebrows, impressed. The kids pick up on that - they experience the realization that their manners affect others positively, and they like that. What's the likelihood they'll remember their manners now? Very, very likely.

My proficiency grew at home schooling *and* at parenting. The close relationship I had built that first year with my children was starting to pay dividends, though with it came endless unexpected responsibilities. The good news was simply that I welcomed them, now, because I so valued the three little lives I was helping define. Aw, who am I kidding? The responsibilities were always there; they were just easier to ignore when the children were at school all day, amiright?

There was a chance that if I'd continued to send Biwa to public school, he might have gotten a fantastic teacher and learned a great deal more than I taught him, but the odds were against that happening. I'd probably have done just as much work with him, during after-school hours and countless other times. At the same time, I'd be trying to undo the negative things he learned from the system and perhaps his peers.

And an 11:15 a.m. finish? Never happen.

Paperwork and Other Distasteful Things

~

Paperwork is part of the process, but it isn't the be-all and end-all that it's cracked up to be. Our over-bureaucratized education system has convinced us that the diploma is the goal, when our purpose really should be a well-rounded, thoughtful, responsible, caring, motivated, and of course educated, young person. A piece of paper only represents a small part of that objective.

One day, early in this venture, I attended an orientation event for a local home school network. A mom had organized this network/school-community several years before. It offered classes, outings, and social events for home-schooled children. The mom who currently ran it spoke about her two disparate children: a daughter who learned to read at two-and-a-half and graduated from college at twenty-two with four degrees, including a law degree, and a son who didn't read until ten but, incredibly, was nearly as accomplished. It's probable that neither of her children would have thrived in a traditional school setting, but they're both well-adjusted, successful individuals today. Her story intrigued and encouraged me.

They held the seminar in an informal setting at a local church. The speaker, another veteran mom of the group, answered many audience questions. I was interested in this 'school,' which provided a "bona fide" diploma and transcript for every graduating student, because of the learning opportunities it offered.

When questions about paperwork began, I was ready to leave, but not because I'm unconcerned. This organization takes pride in being exceedingly disciplined with record keeping, and insists that parents attend a two-day seminar regarding school records. It's probably a good thing, given the current policies and regulations our "free" society lives under. We all must comply with federal and state laws and this also gives member parents a sense of security regarding the validity of the school.

However, many parents are overly concerned with the paperwork. It's understandable, though, because we're brainwashed to expect a good public education and assume it will lead to opportunities and success. We think that a diploma or degree confirms knowledge and value. But current grade inflation has caused diplomas to be worth less than the paper they're written on—a high school diploma may barely get you into college today. Why?

Lifelong Learners

This speaks to an entire world/life view. Colleges that focus on general studies primarily teach students how to be good employees. Many of the most successful people didn't graduate from college. Think Steve Jobs, Bill Gates, and Richard Branson. They're entrepreneurs, people who think out-of-the-box. They aren't employees, people who depend on a small business, a large corporation, or the government, for a paycheck and a retirement account.

College is certainly useful if you want to be a lawyer, a doctor, or an engineer, but it does little to prepare young people for the real world, beyond providing a diploma to carry while seeking employment. The entire 'career readiness' is a catchphrase to mean that once you're done with college, there is no need to learn anything ever again. You are ready to work until you drop! That attitude trickles down to the lower schools as well.

Education should be a lifelong endeavor. People who stop stimulating mental growth have brains that start to atrophy. If we, as a society, allow the focus to be entirely on college – and then getting a good job – we validate the message that education stops where real life begins.

The home schooling method more thoroughly blends education with daily life. It alters the mindset of "go to school to learn, come home to regrettably do homework, and then have the rest of your time unencumbered (and not learning)." Our school happens all the time. It's a way of life. I want my kids to go to college, but only on their own terms, with an end-goal and a plan—not as a way to postpone living fully as adults.

A friend told me he thought of college as a halfway house to real life. I countered that there should be no need for a halfway house, that it was a crutch, and that children should be raised to go off on their own, not to live in some intermediate place between real and sheltered, trying to figure out their next move.

Many young adults are still trying to find themselves while spending copious amounts of money to be educated. After they graduate, they struggle to find meaningful and rewarding careers. How could they? Sadly, they know little of real jobs, having been virtually sequestered inside school walls their entire young lives.

Spinach

At the end of each week in our first year of home school, Biwa composed an essay for grammar and writing. The format changed slightly each week, getting more complex and challenging. I told him that writing was "painting with words" to encourage him. Because he liked putting a paintbrush to paper, I figured this would impress on him the beauty that he could create with words. His blank look indicated otherwise. The writing assignments were often met with tears and complaints, but this particular time, for no apparent reason, he dove into it with enthusiasm.

The topic he chose from the list was why he liked or didn't like a certain food.

What's Wrong with Spinach?
By Biwa Sorbo

I have discovered that I dislike spinach for several reasons. Although many people enjoy eating spinach because it is considered nutritious and beneficial, for me, spinach is the most disgusting vegetable. Spinach's worst offenses are its bad taste, horrible smell, and squishy texture.

One of the reasons I hate to eat spinach is because of its repulsive taste. When I was six, I tried it for the first time and it took four applications of mouthwash to get the taste out of my mouth. Another reason I don't care for spinach is because it smells like a stinky swamp. When my mother made creamed spinach, I almost threw up in my soup! The final reason I abhor [sic] this nasty vegetable is because of its gritty texture. When my mom made me try spinach it stuck to my teeth like tinfoil, making me very uncomfortable.

Spinach has to be the worst vegetable known to mankind. It certainly is for me. There are many foods I like to eat, but spinach is not one of them.

I admit to helping him work out his point, but the intensity and words are all his. I happen to strongly disagree with the sentiments expressed, but the paper certainly stands on its own regarding passion and color. Paint me proud.

The fact is, I could write a similar paragraph about paperwork, which I, wrongfully or rightly, see as false hurdles that I can simply walk around. Forms and files about my children seem so superficial. Lucky for me, the emphasis on paperwork to access a good higher education is changing. More and more universities, even Ivy League ones, are looking intently at home schooled students, so the intense record-keeping may just turn out to be superfluous. I maintain the documentation that my state requires and I keep high school filing for my children, but a few sheets of paper are hardly representative of the individuals. I'm preparing my kids for life-long learning. In some ways, a diploma is like a ticket to a free concert in the park.

Re-Assimilation (Year 2)

~

A friend emailed me to say she'd had an enjoyable winter school holiday but was dreading the whole morning rush back to school.

With our approach, I don't experience that particular phenomenon, although I did wonder how it would go after our long Christmas break. The first week of our three weeks away had no school requirements, and the second two, only minimal reading.

Here's how we re-assimilated.

We arrived home from our trip on Monday morning at 7:30, after a night flight. We were all too exhausted to do any work so I gave them the day off, in exchange for their promise to push everything by a day—meaning schoolwork on Saturday.

Tuesday came and I was still strung out from the lack of sleep and jet-lag, but while I was sitting at my computer first thing in the morning, Biwa waltzed in and started his Latin. "Mom, please print out the assignment sheet, so I can cross things off as I go."

Then he started right into math, and after that, spelling. Finally, he said, "Mom, let's get the grammar done now."

Who was I to say "no" to that? I was way too tired to enforce some sort of work ethic that day, but if he was *asking* me to do grammar, I was, by golly, *gonna* do grammar with him. He ended with history. I'd decided to start him on a new, more comprehensive history curriculum, but suddenly discovered I didn't have all the materials, so I went to the computer and ordered them.

Because of his enthusiasm, the other children followed his example. To answer the question about whether it's difficult to get back to schoolwork after an extended holiday, I'd give a resounding and somewhat surprised, "No!"

On Wednesday, we were back into the swing of things, and by the end of the week, Saturday, we finished our week's studies.

Study and travel

The main challenge was that the next week we were leaving again on Wednesday. Because we'd be joining another family, I didn't want to burden them with too much schoolwork. It's no fun struggling to focus on learning when distracted, and one purpose of our trip was to spend time with other family members. I simply adjusted the plan, taking our math books and a lot to read—the most important element in schooling.

Although we didn't do formal studies during our vacation, I had Biwa reading over an hour each day. We also explored the local historic buildings—a hands-on history lesson.

For Shane, whose reading is challenged, I took my teaching book for reading and we did two lessons each day for about 30-45 minutes. It provided a nice break from the whole doing-nothing-because-you're-on-vacation routine. I also did a few pages from earlier chapters in the same book with Tavia each day. My goal was that by the end of our trip, Shane would be reading.

It worked. When we got back, I took out a level two "I can read" book, one he never could have attempted before my accelerated reading program, and he read it, albeit haltingly. When it came to reading, Shane had an issue with confidence. He excelled in math, so I guessed it was a bit of a trade-off. But after our trip, he was totally reading.

Another wonderful result was that Tavia, four, was now reading three-letter-words with lots of help. Her approach was fearless. She'd say anything—take a stab at a word, even a bold-faced guess—whereas Shane seemed intimidated into silence by the fear of being wrong. No worries. A little cajoling with a bit of encouragement, and he began reading better and better.

Today, after a long time of concentration on the cereal box, he asked, "Mom, does that say 'peanut butter granola' on that box?"

"Yes, Shane. Great job."

Supply and Demand

Welcome to a new year of homeschooling, Sorbo-style.

We started off one week ahead of our public school because we had all really lazed toward the end of the summer, and I knew we'd need a settling-in period. We accomplished this with part-time school using old workbooks to review material and get ready. Meanwhile, I eagerly awaited the arrival of our new textbooks.

We continued with the *Shurley Grammar* curriculum, pursuing years two and four. Biwa hated the writing component, yet he excelled at it. I made a point of noticing how quickly he finished, after he moaned about how long it would take him to do both assignments—he had two on writing days. Shane recoiled from starting, yet actually adored learning and reveled in it once he began.

In mathematics, Shane had the third year Spectrum notebook and Biwa the fourth. They found the books challenging, but not overwhelming. This put Shane, who is two-and- a-half years younger than Biwa, only a year behind him in math, but we never made a big issue of it.

For history, I still liked the series, *The Story of the World*, though the workbooks were a little much for my oldest. He found them too juvenile, and did not enjoy the artwork parts of them, either. I wanted school to be enjoyable, and I certainly couldn't support forcing a child to do what I call busy work, because they also know exactly what that is. Biwa never had patience for drawing or coloring; he lacked both interest and aptitude, so why torture him?

Shane, on the other hand, loved those kinds of things, as well as connect-the-dots and puzzles, so he responded better to the coordinated history workbook. I found him a connect-the-dots book specifically on Egypt and it was all I could do to keep up with him.

As for science, it surrounded us. We had our lizard, Rex, a bearded dragon much akin to a mini tyrannosaurus, and the boys are expert lizard hunters of the smaller indigenous variety. We also tried hatching a tomato hornworm into a moth with one

Shane found after our first four died. The worm eventually formed his chrysalis and buried himself in our terrarium, but not before devouring my tomato plants.

I made a garden this year so the kids got to experience firsthand growing some of the other vegetables they thoroughly dislike. We also attended the Science Night at our public school. I only remembered it at the last minute, after karate, and I innocently asked, "So, do you still want to go to Science Night tonight?

"Yes! I *love* science!" was the resounding answer.

Biwa began studying French this year and had started pronouncing the "R" correctly. I was doggedly researching a better Latin program for the future when it turned out our previous one was only a single year program.

But there were even more important lessons to be learned at home.

Economic Negotiation

I have some very ugly outdoor lights. They're purple and hang very low, giving them a strange vibe. I'd recently realized that if I rehung them upside down, they'd look better. I had asked a painter for a quote to paint them a more palatable color, but never heard back. So, I decided to offer the job to Biwa for a lot more money than he deserved. I thought that by over-rewarding him I'd stimulate a greater sense of responsibility and he might rise to the opportunity. My mistake, but I'm getting ahead of myself, here.

In the beginning he stepped up gamely enough. He took the lanterns I'd removed from the walls, scrubbed and washed them, and then taped them to my satisfaction before starting to paint them with a primer spray paint.

Then his sister made a huge mud puddle with the hose. Shane joined her and that proved too much temptation for Biwa. Mud is fun.

He told me the paint can needed a rest and he was going to join his siblings. He ended up spray-painting his younger brother's arm. I wish I could explain exactly how this occurred, but I wasn't there. They must have had a disagreement, and Biwa grabbed the nearest thing to him and sprayed Shane, who was seven. Livid, I explained that this was completely irresponsible of him—he could have blinded Shane—and I cut his promised wages in half.

But he was only ten. I reconsidered my rush to judgment while he was showering upstairs. When he came downstairs, I told him that perhaps I'd overreacted. I explained I'd only dock his pay by 20%, thus forcing him to do some math as well.

He looked at me with a sly smile. "That's good, Mom, 'cause in the shower I was thinking that I could refuse to do it, and then you'd have to get a guy in to paint and that would cost you a lot of money—more than me." He knew that the painter hadn't returned my calls.

Paint *me* proud, though a little miffed at his cockiness. His barely suppressed glee at having bested me in this negotiation was too obvious to overlook.

After duly absorbing his surprising grasp of basic supply and demand economics, the next day I decided I had to take him down a few pegs. "Biwa, things have changed a bit again."

Then I launched into my revised analysis in a very matter-of-fact tone. "After I applied your logic, I've decided that you're going to do the job for half price. I know that there's nowhere else that you can earn the money I'll pay you, even at this lower amount. So you'll finish the paint job, and be *happy* to collect your pay. If it isn't done today, then I'll do it myself, and that money is off the table for good. And the next time, I hope you'll remember it's best to keep quiet when you're ahead, although I'm very proud of you for thinking the way you did. You are very, very smart!"

Of course he tried to argue with me, but I had the upper hand. How long that will last, I don't know. There's really nowhere else for him to earn that much money, and I know him—he loves money. He eventually agreed, and even put on a smile when I insisted. I enlisted friends to commend his fine job and remark on how well paid he was—not letting on they knew it was only half of our original figure.

This experience provided a couple of tremendously valuable lessons in the art of negotiation and supply and demand—none of which would have been taught in this way had he been enrolled in our local school. (And I'd never have given him this chore with all the homework he'd have been bringing home.)

I also learned a valuable lesson: a child may rise to the occasion you craft for them, but they're only so tall.

ENOUGH

~

We're meant to learn from our children, as the previous story shows. I believe that God created mine specifically for my husband and me. Because of that, I take their education seriously, and as they develop and change, so does their education, and so must I.

Also, as a product of our public education system, myself, I still wrestle with the conviction that someone else can do things better than I can. That attitude pervades our culture today, and even as I observe it with sadness, I can't fully escape it, either.

Our founders held the view that *they* must accomplish all things, if only because there wasn't anyone else to do it for them. Now we do everything for our kids to see that they are educated by the people we believe can do that. When they come home with more work, we do even more for them, to free up some time, so that they can enjoy a bit of their childhoods. I had a masseuse friend, Stella, who never graduated high school. Stella told me her mother used to complete her homework, to avoid embarrassment, instead of spending the extra time needed to help Stella, who was dyslexic, learn. Later, when Mom stopped doing Stella's homework because it got too challenging, Stella stopped performing - it was too late to catch up, and they placed Stella in remedial classes with all the other wash-outs. I said to Stella, "So, the system failed you." "Oh, yes, they failed me," she quickly confirmed. "No," I clarified, "I mean the system totally let you down. Your mom, the school, nobody looked out for you in all that. They failed you." "Well, when you put it that way, I guess you're right. I never figured I could amount to anything." It's an incredibly vicious cycle—and it's all wrong.

Kids slip through the cracks all the time, and we can hardly expect better from our institutions, and yet, I still couldn't escape the idea that maybe I wasn't enough. My children deserve the very best, and in my mind I questioned whether I was the best one to deliver it. I'd never gotten my high school diploma. In my defense, I studied abroad in Sweden my final year of high school, so I missed a few classes needed for graduation. Duke University accepted me before I completed high school, so they were expecting my completed transcript later. It arrived with several Swedish classes on it, but no stamp of completion! And although I performed well at Duke, a wonderful and highly acclaimed university, I didn't finish my schooling there either.

What's a girl to do? No diploma, no degree, just a gaping sense of insecurity, based on those drat papers, which I was raised to acclaim and acquire. My self-doubt plagued me.

I also wanted to give my children a strong Christian upbringing, which I had not received, so once again I pondered, how could I measure up? Although I excelled in math, certainly some teachers were better educated than I in literature and history—of course, there's *always* someone better educated. Self-doubt won the debate, and I decided to try something new.

The year I had Biwa in fourth grade and Shane in second, things were going quite smoothly. The boys were progressing well in their academics: grammar, math, geography, history, French, Bible, spelling, reading, and piano. My daughter, Tavia, was enrolled in our local public school kindergarten, which made her very happy. She had new friends, two girls she adored, and the schedule worked for us, as she started each school day at 11:00.

But I had high anxiety, something home schooling parents everywhere probably struggle with. Were my children learning *enough*? Was I adequate to the task at hand?

A friend of mine, a home school mom, had enrolled her children at a classical Christian academy about a half hour's drive away. She encouraged me to explore this school as a possibility for my boys, and not simply because she wanted a car pool buddy (though I suspect that's at least partly why.) My uncertainty got the best of me and after consulting the headmaster, a highly educated, forthright Christian teacher, I enrolled the boys in their hybrid program: Monday and Tuesday I would home school with the school's curriculum, and Wednesday through Friday would attend the school.

This seemingly perfect solution lasted for eight weeks.

Though I didn't realize it then, I had my answer, my validation, the day before they began, when my boys were assessed. I warned the headmaster that although Shane excelled in math, being a full grade ahead, he wasn't fluent in reading. I assumed he'd score low because of his halting style. I'd worked hard with him over that previous vacation and he'd made real progress. I thought I'd just brought him up to a remedial level, and in my assessment, he hadn't improved much since then.

Testing would be a good measure of his standing and the headmistress of the school was intent on finding out exactly where she should place Shane. She disappeared with little Shane for about twenty minutes, as I waited with bated breath for her judgment. I was actually nervous. Was I a bad teacher? Mother? Suffice it to say my insecurity was full-tilt or I wouldn't have been there in the first place. Now I was really putting my accomplishments with my kids on display, looking for approbation of any sort, expecting... What was I expecting? Certainly not the results I received.

She returned with Shane. "Well, you're right about his math. He's definitely proficient at least a grade higher than his age, but we can handle that by putting him in the older class. As for his reading..." She paused.

I waited for the boom to come down on my shame.

"Shane's reading at a fourth grade level," she said with a twinkle in her eye.

I hesitated over this unexpected good information. "So... I'm the one with the problem?"

"Pretty much;" She smiled.

Tears sprang to my eyes. I *wasn't* a lousy teacher, after all. I briefly basked in the sunshine of my success.

Quality and Quantity Time

Do the math. Assume a teacher devotes equal time to each student she has during the six hours in the classroom. After deducting lunch and playground time, that leaves roughly five hours. If a class has thirty students, that averages out to ten minutes per student. Because they teach a lot of kids at once, it appears to be a more efficient way to get the job done. It would be, if children were little robots, ready for programming, but they aren't. The argument seems to be that the children learn more when the teacher addresses them as a group. That theory assumes that students have no upper limit to the amount they can absorb in a day, and therefore only benefit from longer days and more instruction, while being deprived of one-on-one attention.

Humans thrive with human touch. In fact, studies show that babies who are deprived of human interactions exhibit all kinds of learning limitations. For instance, children from orphanages, with minimal contact, tend to perform poorly in school, compared with children from intact families. "Many children who have not had ample physical and emotional attention are at higher risk for behavioral, emotional and social problems as they grow up."[78]

The school model severely restricts their exposure to one-on-one child-adult interaction. The need for adult contact does not dissipate as soon as infants learn to walk. Some government types argue for providing preschool for all children, which would detrimentally deprive them of their parents earlier in their lives. Heaven forbid.

One famous study showed that preschool children read much earlier than others who didn't attend preschool. It was later debunked when those same children lost all their advantages by second grade. In *Study: States' Methods for Rating Preschool Quality Fail to Predict Children's Readiness for Kindergarten*, Audrey Breen[79] writes, "However, researchers at the University of Virginia, Northwestern University and the University of North Carolina, Chapel Hill isolated one factor of the many used in the rating systems that did make a difference in school readiness: the quality of teacher-student interactions."

Terri J. Sabol, postdoctoral fellow at the Institute for Policy Research at Northwestern, confirmed, "Children who were in classrooms with higher ratings based on *observed interactions between teachers and students* were more prepared for kindergarten." (Emphasis mine) Adult-child interactions were the only differentiating factor in kindergarten academic preparedness for children.

Back to my story: I shouldn't have been surprised that Shane tested as advanced. I had, after all, given him one-on-one instruction with love and affection, and lots of praise. It was me who didn't understand that second graders typically are not completely fluent when they read aloud. Ah, but it would be a while before I finally did comprehend that my insecurities were my own worst enemy.

I enrolled the boys because I'd concluded that I was inferior, that others were better equipped, more educated, and had greater experience with kids. I assumed they'd have better teachers despite the evidence of my success.

My low self-confidence made decision making hard for me. I regularly weigh each option and do hours of research. I look at ingredients and labels in the supermarket and do price calculations. When it came to school, my research suggested this would work, and once that difficult decision was made, I had no interest in revisiting it. I took the new information in, but adhered to my (now) old conclusion—I had a plan, and was sticking to it.

Both boys attended for those first few weeks, and over that time my aggravation with the "system" grew. As good a job as the educators there were doing, I realized Shane was no longer at liberty to pursue his mathematics to his heart's content. Now he was on a treadmill, along with his entire class.

I had the kids for Mondays and Tuesdays at home, where we would do the assigned work. Then on Wednesdays through Fridays they would be in the classrooms with the other kids. About half the kids there were on this hybridized school schedule.

The teacher often sent work via email or downloadable file. Once, I couldn't download the files. It turned out to be a glitch and the files weren't available by the day they were due, Monday. The teacher emailed. "Don't worry about it, it isn't that important."

I was disappointed. If she assigned it, why was it suddenly unimportant? Her comment made their homework seem like busywork, something I abhor. Kids are pretty smart. They know when it's work without a good purpose and I suspected that's what it was. It bothered me, but for a one-time occurrence, I let it go. After that I paid close attention to things sent home. Some seemed superfluous, but overall, it was the delivery system that was flawed and frustrating.

School terms were divided into six-week periods, so, after the initial six weeks, I asked to meet with the teachers to discuss the boys' progress. Insecure again, I wanted to know if I was pulling my weight in our deal of the hybridized school weeks.

I met with Shane's teacher first. She immediately focused on how well he behaved in class. She raved about how quiet he was, that she seated the most rambunctious boy next to him in the hopes Shane would have a calming effect on that little boy, which he did, and how happy she was with the results of her experiment.

I was unimpressed, to say the very least. Shane's behavior was, in fact, the lowest on my list of concerns. I realized that teachers are, in fact, traffic control cops, and so my son was simply good at being herded. "What about his academics?"

"He's doing fine..."

"Fine" was an unacceptable accolade, when I'd seen him love learning at home.

Home Again

Biwa started to come home with this oldest-child attitude again, belittling and teasing his younger siblings. The curriculum was not, as I had imagined, tremendously better than mine. And if I had to have one more discussion about the carpool schedule, which was more complicated than the new health care bill, I knew it would be the final straw for my sanity.

I determined to pull them out again, and told them. Strangely, they took it in stride. They were curious, of course, asking why and listening intently to my explanation that I didn't feel like they were getting what I wanted them to have from a school experience. They both nodded gravely. I think the whole waking up early, making their lunches, organizing books and the hour minimum travel each day was aggravating them, too. On their last day of school, Shane bounded into the kitchen to announce, "Mommy, I'm so happy today is my last day of school!"

As we settled back into our old routine, Shane began complaining that he didn't understand his math.

I was mystified. *Where did that come from?*

He cried. "It's too hard for me."

"Of course it isn't," I assured him. "You're brilliant in math. Let's do it together."

I don't know what had made him fear math, although the text they used *was* about four inches thick, and a book that size would put *me* on edge. It took six weeks to undo his apprehension, so he could enjoy math again.

I'm still working with Biwa on not bullying his siblings with derogatory comments and controlling behaviors. But the boys are happier at home and I'm happier to have them here. Biwa often asks to be wakened at six, so he can be done with school before nine.

Ultimately, I learned several lessons: I'm not much of a team player when it comes to the education of my children; I'm more like long-distance runner. I can't outsource my kids' schooling, and luckily, I don't need to. I am an effective teacher. It's good for my youngest to view her siblings hunkering down to get their school work done, though at times without the happiest of smiles, but with a satisfied resolve and energy for the task.

I finally received the validation I craved, so I could begin to relax. Our kids' education is so important, and so many little things can affect them at this tender age. I am incredibly happy to know that I can supervise and protect them myself, and help them grow into responsible, fearless young adults. That's enough.

And so am I.

INSECURITY (YEAR 3)

~

Choosing to home school invites insecurity as a constant companion. Can one ever measure up to a government institution that has been practicing and perfecting the art and science of schooling children for over a century?

Over recent decades, home scholars have answered that question with a resounding "yes!" In fact, many of those students have surpassed the government's standards, inadvertently highlighting the general inadequacies of our learning institutions.

Two factors are significant:

1. *Home schoolers refused to compromise their principles.*
2. *Bureaucracies have limitations.*

The government can't serve all children equally, because each child is unique. Therefore, they adopt a plan that levels the expectations, by slowing down the better performers. Although this approach may seem counter-intuitive, it's much easier to hold back the advanced students than try to accelerate the less gifted ones. In stark contrast, home schooling parents can focus on the strengths of each child to provide appropriate material and extra assistance as needed, breaking the yoke of the public school agenda.

My eyes were truly opened after briefly enrolling my two boys in that very qualified private school.

Although they used the same *Shurley Grammar* curriculum, the extremely repetitive writing program was painfully intense for their students. In all honesty, it was challenging for my boys as well. The headmaster explained to me that it wasn't necessary to adhere so strictly to the material. The school supplanted *Shurley's* writing program with another plan from *Institute for Excellence in Writing* (IEW). They also chose to not complete everything in *Shurley's* grammar segment.

This disturbed my obsessive, exigent self. *What if they missed something?* I calmed myself with the realization that things missed would be covered later, during the inevitable repetition that exists as a natural way of reinforcing concepts and methods.

Teachers rarely cover textbooks in their entirety whether in private or public schools. I recall my mother's horror when she discovered our high school biology class only covered 17 of 56 chapters. Wow. That seemed like a lot of missed material, and it probably was. My mother unceremoniously moved the entire family from that school system to a better rated one across town.

Because I remember that, when I found out I could also choose to skip some material in a curriculum, I did a little research. Most curricula are purposely over-written; giving teachers limited autonomy and the ability to pick and choose, and also to keep advanced children busy with extra work. Average or slower students never see (or need to see) the extra stuff—what can sometimes be called "busy work."

If revered institutions don't complete the textbooks, why was I holding myself to such a high standard? Because I'm a perfectionist… but that's unhealthy for my kids and me. I decided that just because I have high standards *doesn't* mean I must follow and complete an *entire* curriculum to find educational satisfaction.

Keep your eye on the ball. *Learning* is the goal, the textbook is just a tool.

Year three

My third year, I relaxed a bit. I did *most* of the *Shurley* sentences for each lesson, and about a third of the writing assignments. Because *Shurley* is repetitive, I reasoned there would be plenty of writing the following year, and justifiably. Children learn best through repetition. They often can't grasp an entire concept at one sitting, but need many exposures to complicated ideas, like how to write a particular kind of essay.

They shouldn't be subjected to tedious busy work to instill information that will be covered many times. There *is* a fine line. But at the risk of losing them to boredom or frustration, I err on the side of caution—everything in moderation. We cover the basics until I see they understand, confident that review is coming. This way, the loves of my life aren't burdened with *my* obsessive perfectionism, agonizing to complete tomes of structured learning. I'd rather we concentrate on enjoying the process instead.

I've learned to deal with my insecurity, which goes hand-in-hand with my perfectionism. Sometimes it's quite challenging, but I've found a balance between my desire to fulfill every single demand of an over-written schoolbook and the broad strokes of the public schools. As long as my kids excel, enjoy the process, and can show my husband how to diagram a sentence with an object compliment adjective, that's a successful result for me.

In the summer of 2013, I decided to become a classical tutor for *other* people's children. Wow. That was quite a shift!

The previous year, I had started with a group called Classical Conversations, which involved meeting one day each week with member-families, and a tutor for the children, who adhered to a set curriculum. The younger children had only three hours of instruction, and the parents were required to remain in the classroom with their children. Having participated the previous year with my kids as attendees, I'd fully embraced it. I love what it inspires and the strategies it employs. It challenges students, teachers, and parents just enough, but not too much. The rest of the days at home, we reviewed what was covered in class and I embellished it with my own chosen material. It was, for me, the perfect fit.

I loved the Classical Conversations model. It is a curriculum that follows the classical Christian education method, providing limited input in the early years, slightly more for the late-grammar years, and then a full curriculum starting at the equivalent of seventh grade.

A few things convinced me to ramp up my participation to become a tutor. First, we'd enjoyed an excellent experience the previous year. Second, I was desperate to find out who'd be tutoring my oldest for the six, hour-long seminars one day each week. Every time I asked, my lovely program director would respond with a special gleam in her eye, "I don't know, but I'm certain somebody great will turn up." She'd smile sweetly, probably to hide her secret. She intended it to be me.

Finally, I prayed about it and decided that to run screaming *from* this incredible and awesome burden *and* opportunity — it looked so *hard* — was precisely the reason I *should* volunteer. I was thrilled and excited beyond belief, honored that other discerning parents deemed me fit to advise them and their young children.

I would guide the children one day each week in all their studies and come alongside parents in their home endeavors.

I knew it wouldn't be easy, tutoring a class of ten seventh-graders in the Classical Conversations (CC) program. In a seminar class, a small group of students and a tutor sit around a table, which encourages interaction and discussion. The model welcomes debate and challenges the students to contribute. You can't hide in a class of ten. (The largest class size for CC is twelve.)

Lesson from College

When I began at Duke University, I was required to take American History (because I needed it to graduate high school, and hadn't had it my senior year — in Sweden.) The choices ranged from "history for jocks" to overwhelming upper-level classes. Some people warned me away from a seminar with a stodgy old dean because seminar classes were more difficult, requiring students to perform in the intimate discussion group setting. There would be no skating by, half asleep, with blank homework pages in a class of ten students. Of course, I chose his course. I knew I needed a challenge.

Early in life I'd learned to choose the hard thing, because boredom was worse than hard work, and often led to worse grades. American History was incredibly boring to me. I hoped this would be more stimulating than stifling, and was rewarded by perhaps the best course in my whole time at Duke.

The dean was an ordained minister, something about which I had no opinion at the time. I wasn't a believer and had no use for religion. Though I recall no discussions about God in the classroom, I have little doubt that his religiosity informed his delicate guidance of the class and promoted a better understanding in his students of the deeply religious men who formed this nation.

He gave us plenty of opportunities for conversation and dispute, and left me with a true appreciation of history that had previously eluded me. We recreated historic debates in class, an exciting way to learn. I understood, more than anything, that these were real people struggling to make a better life for themselves and for us, their descendants. I'm forever grateful for that experience, because I gained a solid understanding of the incredible legacy of this country. Ultimately, though, the seminar style and small class size held me personally accountable, which afforded me the experience of learning actively (not passively, as in lectures) and incentivized me to engage more in my own education.

Benefits of Shared Education

Education doesn't happen in a vacuum. Like tourism, it's better when shared. That's hard to achieve with thirty kids the same age, but not necessarily the same educational level. Seminars offer a more tailored and personal experience with increased accountability.

Now I would be teaching in that environment. My excitement rose, as I considered that my students would study the classics — books that would challenge them to think, consider, and justify.

The classical model is superior to some other education systems in part because it relies on time-tested literature. I've often argued for the use of the classics and classical language as a basis for instruction. However, I've never expressed it as succinctly and beautifully as this home schooling mother who works for the Classical Conversations organization.

> *"By reading the classics, we initiate children into adulthood. We train them to exercise their reason on fictional issues so that they may be able to exercise discernment and sound judgment in their own lives. Reading great books and entering the great conversation that has continued throughout history is a critical part of maturing to both the love of wisdom and the practice of virtue."* [80]

Jennifer Courtney was responding to a mother who contended that kids should simply read what they enjoy. That's like offering them what they want for dinner — and the green M&M's are healthier, right?

It reminded me of a statement by our local superintendent of schools deriding the necessity of learning long division, because, well, calculators! Extrapolate that perspective to why learn anything at all? Computers can do everything these days, am-I-right? (Never mind who creates the computers and their programs...)

The *reason* we learn is to be able to make our own choices and decisions. The State's intent for education is to make *productive workers. Career readiness and job preparedness*, remember? These are two nearly mutually exclusive purposes: self-determination versus subordinating the individual to their employment. One upholds freedom while the other espouses virtual slavery. Education is the foundation of freedom. Knowledge and reason provide the crucial components for citizens to act responsibly in sustaining our great country, yet schools today affirm work as the highest good, and to that end, assign the most outrageous reading materials.

A discerning mind might conclude that the government is acting against the interests of personal liberty and individual responsibility. Common sense rejects the notion that freedom should be relinquished at the offer of a food stamp and a Band-Aid. To accept these items is not unreasonable, but the easy choice is rarely the best choice. We shouldn't permit government "experts" to control various aspects of our lives. Acquiescing to that is easy cowardice.

Sometimes, you have to do something that's hard simply because it *is* hard—to practice, to build strength. Often the difficult decision is the right one. If you go to the gym but don't lift the weights, you won't get strong. Similarly, children need appropriate challenges to learn to analyze and to draw conclusions, to avoid ending up unequipped, weak, and stupid.

The classical model requires students read challenging literature because that's how they grow, learn to think, and hone their ability to reason. According to the classical model, teaching is the final stage of learning, the opportunity to exercise knowledge of the material. I can attest to that, having finally truly learned calculus as I tutored it in college.

My seminar encouraged the students to challenge each other, including me. I grew and gained insight in the process, right along with them. One of my favorite lines of study was of apologetics. The moment I saw that as part of a seventh-grade curriculum, I rejoiced. How brilliant, I thought! I told my friend, wryly, "Why don't they teach this in high school?" She countered, seriously, "Why don't they teach that in church youth group?" Equipping our kids to defend their faith is exactly what they need in this all-too secular world. Think about that. If you want your children to have any knowledge of God, understand that one hour a week of weak instruction at church is no hedge against the anti-God surroundings in a public school. They teach evolution, which is equivalent to 'survival of the fittest.' Is it any wonder kids shoot up schools? They won't teach the Bible in school, although it is a phenomenal history text. These positions are anti-church. So, again, if you want your kids growing up with faith, how can you, in good conscience, send them to any non-religious school?

The other courses I was to tutor were also very much to my liking, including the Saxon math course. Initially, I balked at the very large, thick math tome. Ugh! That brought me back to my days in high school when I refused to carry my math book home and therefore never did my math homework. I had a three mile walk each way, and that book was really too heavy! But, I had made a commitment, and *Saxon Math* was part of the deal. Once I started into the Saxon text, however, my reservations faded away.

Some of my fondest memories of my time tutoring seventh grade are our math time in class.

Raising children is difficult. Many of us find ourselves overwhelmed by all the challenges children can pose. But doing the hard thing is often the only responsible way forward. I've tried to show that as hard as it is, it's still not as hard as sending your kids *away from you* to the state institution to be educated.

FAITH

~

This book wouldn't be complete without a discussion of the role of faith in education, and not simply because, let's face it, if you decide to home school your children, that is a leap of faith!

I chose to educate my offspring with the Classical Christian model, because it has time-tested success and the *trivium*, on which it is based, made more sense to me than the education I grew up with. Current education is divided into 'subjects', which all seem disparate. The classical model showed me they are, in fact, all interrelated. I began lamenting my own education. If only I'd been taught that words were like numbers, and sentences were like equations, just somewhat more free. Science cannot be learned, really learned, outside its historical context, and history can't be truly understood without solid comprehension of, well, everything else. What good is knowing about Archimedes' Screw Pump if I simply regard it as outdated? The Classical Method ties all the various 'subjects' together, like spokes on a grand wheel, at the center of which is God the Creator. Suddenly, the world makes sense. What follows this is that the student begins to appreciate his or her defined, sensible role in the world, and cannot simply perceive himself or herself as a lucky (or unlucky) accident. With this type of education, *life takes on meaning*, even for the youngest student.

Education used to be religiously motivated and devoted to training up the faithful. It used to be concerned with instilling wisdom. Today, especially in public schools, faith has been relegated to a footnote, replaced with secularism, which is its own belief-system, and belief in God has become a side-topic often spoken about with derision.

Our second president, John Adams, said, "Our Constitution was made only for a moral and religious people. It is wholly inadequate to the government of any other."[81]

Without a morally principled society, our laws are ineffective and useless, paving the way for tyranny. That's the pragmatist's argument for teaching Judeo-Christian ethics to our children. Our country was founded on these principles and cannot survive without them. Currently, we are living off the moral capital inherited from our cultural ancestors, but that's running out.

Consider the painting of Jesus that an Ohio high school removed after the American Civil Liberties Union threatened a lawsuit. The beautiful piece of art, hung in 1971 in memory of a beloved teacher, suddenly became offensive. It was a painting. If you think the school system isn't aggressively persecuting and purging the schools of Christianity, think again.

Recently, I saw an email from someone who works for the Minnesota school system. She received a package, addressed to the schools, from CAIR, the Council for American-Islamic Relations, which included a letter (see Appendix), together with a Koran. They expressed their intent to provide a better "mutual understanding between our cultures."

Why is there no feminist group arguing that the hijab, the sometimes-traditional Muslim headwear for women, should not be forced on women because it isn't required for men? So much for equal rights. Few speak out about the atrocities visited on young Muslim girls and women every day, female genital mutilation and honor killings, which even happen in the US. These are examples of the lack of freedom under Islamic law, which proves that unreformed Islam's Shari'a law is anathema to the basic tenets of our American legal system and the Judeo-Christian way of life.

In Tempe, Arizona, a high school mandated that all female students wear the hijab for an entire month, because a young Muslim woman was bullied in the bathroom.[82] While bullying is wrong, and it appears they targeted her because of her headscarf, how is making the entire student body wear headscarves going to *correct* bullying behavior? And why doesn't the mandate include all the male students, as well? I would argue this is teaching the students intolerance, not the opposite.

One parent commented about the new mandate, "I heard what happened to that girl, and yes, it was wrong. But what if a kid gets bullied for being fat? Are we going to force all the students to eat cupcakes? This is absurd, and it isn't Christian."

While the ACLU tries to further expunge Christianity from our education system, CAIR infiltrates it to instill respect for Islam. In a seventh-grade classroom in Tennessee, the heart of the Bible belt, students were instructed to write, "There is no God but Allah; Muhammad is the Messenger of Allah."[83] We fought our costliest war to end slavery and now we're asked to accept that same practice in the name of diversity.

In Michigan, tenth-grade students are instructed to design a booklet to teach Islam to third-graders, putting them in the position of advocates. One parent posted her reaction to the assignment on Facebook:

> *"I can't comprehend why prayer is not allowed in school, but teaching [any] religion is? What happened to separation of church and state? By requiring my daughter to make a pamphlet promoting another god, they are violating my religious beliefs. Also, they are presenting false information about who Allah is."* [84]

With breathtaking hubris, the principal went on record, saying of Ms. Hall's post that "unfortunately, a lot of times in today's society, information is spread very quickly without maybe knowing all the facts." [84]

The story is quite clear: Islam is *in*, and Christianity is *out*. Even some evangelicals oppose teaching the Bible in school, claiming it won't be given the gravitas it deserves.[85] I disagree. The Bible is the best history book known to man, and it is filled with wisdom as well. The problem arises with the teachers, though, and how they would teach the lessons in the Bible. Because *everything* is always open to interpretation, though, I side with using the

Bible, as opposed to some other text. Roma Downey and Mark Burnett, producers of "The Bible" TV series, agree:

> *Have you ever sensed in your own life that "the handwriting was on the wall"? Or encouraged a loved one to walk "the straight and narrow"?*
>
> *Have you ever laughed at something that came "out of the mouths of babes"? Or gone "the extra mile" for an opportunity that might vanish "in the twinkling of an eye"?*
>
> *If you have, then you've been thinking of the Bible.*
>
> *These phrases are just "a drop in the bucket" (another biblical phrase) of the many things we say and do every day that have their origins in the most read, most influential book of all time. The Bible has affected the world for centuries in innumerable ways, including art, literature, philosophy, government, philanthropy, education, social justice and humanitarianism.* [86]

For these reasons and more, many support reintroducing the Bible into our schools. In fact, there is a project now to use the Bible as a history textbook. [87] Their website claims, "The program was designed to address the fact that, without an understanding of the Bible, today's youth cannot fully understand literature, art, history, music or culture." Ain't that the truth!

Historical Faith

The founders knew that one day each week at church wasn't enough. They practiced their religion every day, and it was an integral part of their children's education. The Bible was the main textbook back then, but no longer. It takes a daily plan to counter the secular cultural trends that are reinforced continually at our schools.

Thomas Jefferson instituted prayer in the Capitol Rotunda, yet when children study him today, they are often informed he was a religious skeptic, a deist - not a Christian — subtly suggesting that if Jefferson didn't believe, why should they? The same is indicated about the other founder, George Washington. Of the other fifty-four founders who signed the Declaration of Independence, twenty-nine held what would be considered seminary or Bible school degrees. Their overwhelming religiosity is all but ignored by our public schools.

When religion is addressed in our schools, our Judeo-Christian heritage is downplayed. However, Islam enjoys more leniencies and is viewed tolerantly, as a favored minority. This is both wrong-headed and dangerous. Secularism enjoys a tacit understanding of being simply a lack of religion. Nothing could be further from the truth! Even Wikipedia lists Secularism/Atheism/Agnosticism as the world's third largest religion, because it is a competing world-view, one untethered to morals and principles as defined by nature and nature's law. Secularism espouses survival of the fittest, not the sanctity of life. Sadly, Christians ceded the school grounds to secularism long ago.

An acquaintance was sending her son to college. I said, "Be careful. The colleges these days indoctrinate the kids away from their religion. He may come back an atheist!" I was only half joking, but she shrugged me off. "He's been in Catholic church his entire life. Wednesdays and Sundays! He's a good Catholic boy. Nothing's going to change with that, trust me." Four years later, her son moved back into town no longer a believer. His faith had been tested, shaken, and dislodged. She was, of course, distraught. It's a wonder, but even the full churchgoing time spent in his childhood wasn't inoculation enough against the derision and aggressive anti-God stance of the secular college.

Tragedy

There's an excellent documentary called *Indoctrination* in which Brian Rohrbough, a divorced parent, tells the story of the last time he saw his son, Daniel. He had dinner with Daniel and they shared a little time together before he dropped him off back at his mother's home, like many other occasions.

Daniel said, "I love you, Dad. I'll see you tomorrow," and went up to the front door.

Brian looked up after backing out of the driveway, to see Daniel waving with a big smile.

The following morning, April 20th, Brian received a call from his panic-stricken ex-wife, asking if he had heard from Dan. "Do you know what's going on?" she asked. Then she relayed to him the reports of two gunmen who had entered Columbine High School with machine guns and hand grenades. They were killing students.

Brian rushed to the school, but never saw his son until the following day. That morning, he opened the newspaper and saw Daniel's body, wearing his green shirt and blue jeans, lying dead on the school sidewalk. It was his only notification.

Brian, a Christian, admitted in the film that he was weakly lukewarm on most issues:

> *I knew how bad the public schools were, and I knew that because I was in the public schools. And as parents we want to believe that things have gotten better, when in fact they have gotten much worse.*
>
> *As a parent it was my responsibility to make sure that my son was safe, that he was educated properly, but I failed that. I put him in a pagan school, where they teach them that there is no God, there is no Creation, there's evolution based on a cosmic accident, and evolution breaks down to one simple belief: that the strong kill the week as a form of survival and that there's nothing wrong with that.*
>
> *It is a worldview religion, it is an atheistic religion, and yet it is taught in the school. And I put my son there, even though I am a Christian. So, when we talk about my son's murder, yes, it's right to condemn these two murderers, it is right to condemn the school system that taught these wicked things. But you must remember, I am the one who put him there.*

The film reports that since Daniel Rohrbough's death at Columbine there were over 400 school-associated violent deaths in this country.

School's surround our children with an ideology that is deadly to them, if not physically, then at least spiritually. We lament that the Columbine children didn't stand a chance against the weapons fired at them. In a similar way, children in secular schools stand little chance against the ideas of the non-religious and anti-religious, who believe strongly in the absence of any God, and in the government as the provider and arbiter of right and wrong, in other words, the survival of the fittest.

Once you decide to take charge of your kids' education, there are several options open to you, but the sooner you recognize that dropping them off at a government institution does not absolve you of your responsibilities, and does not benefit them as much you might have originally thought, the better. If you're at all like Kevin and me, your children are probably the most precious things in your life. They represent your hopes and dreams, the future, and the best parts of you. Keep them close.

After all, they're *your* kids.

Questions?

~

For some, the decision to home school is almost too daunting to consider. I've presented in this book the arguments proving that the alternative of public school is even more so! If you don't have a good Christian school option (and even if you do), I urge you to face your fears and dig in to what probably be the very best adventure of your adult life — educating your children. Here are some questions and responses that I've come across in my endeavors.

1) *How could I home educate? I'm not capable!* The question is, if you graduated from your public high school, maybe even a good college, and ended up incapable of instructing nine-year-olds, what hope do you hold for your children who you send to public schools? Education should be contagious, not constrictive. Doesn't your own sense of inadequacy compel you to protect your children from enrolling them in the same kind of institution that clearly, by your own tacit admission, failed you?
2) *Where do I start?* Now, you're talking! If you have children, you've already begun. Congratulations!
3) *How do I know what to teach?* There is a list of resources at the back of this book, and plenty of information online, as well as through clubs and other home schoolers. You are not alone!
4) *Why should I bother? It's so much work!* Not when you recognize that doing homework is home schooling — just at the end of the day, when everyone is tired and cranky and hungry. When you do homework with your student, you are already accepting responsibility

for the education of your child, and acknowledging the limitations of a government institution that has admitted it cannot perform adequately. Congratulations!

5) *The schools in my district are excellent!* Compared to what? Certainly not compared to a caring parent and the accountability he or she requires.
6) *I can't possibly do the math!* Neither can the school teachers, adequately enough for each child. That's why all these math-tutoring places have sprouted up everywhere. Textbooks do an excellent job of explaining. Have more faith in your abilities, especially with grade school mathematics.
7) *I work full-time.* For parents who work full-time, there are many creative solutions to solving the school puzzle. For instance, if you do homework with your child, you are already home-schooling them. Consider hiring a retired teacher, and devoting a little time to determining the proper curricula for them to pursue with your child. This gives you autonomy, without demanding your minute-by-minute participation. There are also school co-ops that may be interested in having you join them, and older children can benefit from online school options as well, which have requirements to keep students on track.
8) *What about socialization?* School should be about education. Socialization is secondary to the main goal. But it is important, and home schooled children are, in general, much better socially because they customarily deal more often with adults and children of other ages than school kids in age-biased classrooms for seven hours each day.
9) *I just need time for myself sometimes!* Home schooling requires, on average for middle-upper grade school, three hours per day *from the student.* That still leaves plenty of time for you. But if you really want to be

alone, send the kid to school. You may end up more alone than you desire, later in life.

10) *What are the guarantees?* There are no guarantees in life. There is only agreement that US schools and the educational bureaucracy is broken. The good news is this means the bar is really low, and you, with your child, can step over it easily.

I hope hesitation seems ludicrous when compared to the issues with today's schooling that I've outlined in this book. Are you still willing to blindly accept the public school treadmill that society condones? I have a secret about home schooling your children that I'd like to share:

It's not as hard as you think.

There are so many options online these days for schooling. The home schooling community has exploded with curriculum. Public schools have gotten into the business, by offering K-12 online or home school-for-free plan. Some organizations will even pay you (for the pleasure of getting your tax <education> dollars); they offer a modest stipend in exchange for your child's enrollment, enough to take the kid to museums and such throughout the year.

When people find out I home school, they often ask, "What's it really like? Isn't it hard?"

I have to smile. The short answer is "No!" You have to live it to believe it. We've all been indoctrinated that our bricks-and-mortar public schools are necessary, to the point that *socialization* is currently the best excuse some people have for sending their kids. "My children just crave being around their friends." Well, if we let the children decide what they prefer to do… I have absolutely no interest in sending my kids to school to socialize for eight hours a day, and then have them bring home the work that *should have been done at school.*

Great Relationships with Your Children

One wonderful result of home schooling is the connection that you can have with your child. This can be a fantastic, rewarding relationship, where you regularly listen to each other. On the other hand, sending your child to school for eight hours a day will improve absolutely nothing in your relationship.

Home schooling is so easy that it's hard to mess it up. Your child could likely skip an entire year of grade school and return the following year with little to no problem because so much that happens in a public school classroom, and in education in general, is repetition. My fourth grader is doing again the same grammar that my second grader is covering. His is a bit more in-depth, but they are both looking at possessives—something many adults struggle with. My second-grader typically asks to do some of his older sibling's math problems because he likes the challenge they present.

Compare school to buying a house. You walk through it and love it. The inspector says it's great, the neighborhood is right, and so you purchase it. You may not realize until after you've moved in that the roof leaks or that it's drafty. (Inspectors have disclaimers in their contracts for such things.)

You can repair the roof or apply caulking. (Hire a tutor.) The draftiness is caused by a faulty design of the heating system. Buy a few sweaters. (Hire a therapist for the kid.)

But eventually you discover the house's foundation is defective and twelve years later (graduation) the building starts to sink. (Your child can't hold a job, because of low self-esteem, or high self-esteem, and no one taught him anything about the skills needed to hold one, or, worse, he doesn't even know to *desire* independence, because the government education bureaucracy taught him to revere the government-as-provider. His education was steeped in entitlement, recycling, and nature conservation.)

Luckily, a good homeowner's insurance policy covers the foundation issues.

But little will mitigate the deficits in your child's education. He's moving back home.

The future of our children is at stake, and parents have blindly entrusted the care of their kids to those who, on a broad scale, have proven to be mediocre, at best. Would you knowingly hire an average or less-than-average builder to construct your home? Are your children more valuable than your home?

Frail excuses to avoid home schooling abound: it's too scary, it requires too much work, or it's too risky. These objections don't address the real issue. Instead, we should be wondering if we can afford *not* to home school. Because we've been served a brew of Common Core without a warning label, *this* is a warning to those who can make the change to home schooling, but hesitate. Now that you know what's in the punch, think twice about drinking it.

Options

There are a great many different ways to home educate, but requirements vary by state. If you're a die-hard conformist, you can do public school online. This often requires reporting to a local teacher/advisor. Or, you can join a co-op or a group and sign your child up for classes and field trips, with some classes taught by other parents. If your older child is capable, there are community college classes available. I have a friend whose nine-year-old took Trigonometry at the local college last year.

Recently I was on the phone with a new acquaintance, and she discovered that we home school. She said, "I always thought about that, but I'd have to make so many adjustments... I don't know. It's too scary to even think about."

Too frightening to consider?

I encouraged her. "Do your research. It's not that scary. Educate yourself before you write it off, because five years from now, you really don't want to be sitting there wondering why you didn't bother."

Even if you just decided to take a year off from school for your child — just to work on your relationship, when she went back to school the following year, she would likely catch up pretty easily. When I was in fifth grade I got a pass in English for an entire semester because they were repeating the previous year's content, and I had aced the assessment.

So if you're wondering, but are still afraid or unsure, know there are a lot of other people who observed that public school simply wasn't *good enough*, and felt compelled to offer their children an alternative. Then take the plunge, reminding yourself, "I could do worse—and leave them in public school."

READY, SET, GO!

~

Now that you've finished my story and seen the tragedy of sending your children to an institution for long days, only to have them come home with work to do, here's some quick advice on how to get started with a Common Sense world view.

Do some research; get empowered!

1) Find out how you're legally allowed to home school in your state, and what the parameters are. There are several resources online, including the Home School Legal Defense Association, which offers home school insurance and state-specific information, that I highly recommend.

2) Join a home school group for support. There may be several in your area, or there may only be one or two. You may even need to start your own, but mutual assistance and support is a helpful part of this grand undertaking. Remember, the system is against you, working constantly in the media and social networks. I had several mentors who gave me advice and encouragement when I was first considering home schooling and after I had started. I still have many people I look up to for sound counseling.

3) Go to a convention or attend a seminar. There are many different conventions held around the country and they're worth the trip. People with a wide variety of backgrounds attend and support

the home school community. Seminars offer a wealth of advice on the outlook and application of home school philosophies. Overall, these are events filled with the uplifting message that you aren't alone (or crazy), and that is worth the price of admission.

4) Start researching curricula. I highly recommend the classical Christian method, which, of course, has a Christian worldview. If this isn't your cup of tea, there are many other options, although I, personally, would recommend avoiding anything specifically labeled Common Core (or anything popular in public schools, unless you fully vet it). Some of the math programs have been aligned to the CCSSI. Sometimes the changes are minor, but in other sources, the changes are quite sobering. If you want to raise a child with patriotism and a sense of self-worth, avoid CCSSI history and English recommendations, certainly. The simplest approach would be to pass up any texts that are labeled CCSSI compliant. Another option, and one that I personally love, is to get older textbooks - ones from early last century, or before, for any subject matter that stands the test of time, like math and distant history.

I've compiled a very limited resource list, from my personal experience, to provide some information about what's going on in our school system, as well as get you started on your home education journey. Learn more about why and how our schools are massively failing, then the steps you can take to move away from that stagnating atmosphere and into a better world. This list is by no means exhaustive! It is simply a very few of my recommends to parents new to home education, and there are a plethora of other excellent resources out there to inform and guide you. As for curriculum, I am reluctant to get too far down into the weeds. Including the few I mention in this book, the choices of good teaching materials out there is vast. Enjoy the hunt!

My list of recommends begins with documentaries, because we inhabit such a visual, immediate culture. Documentary films can be boring — but not these! In less than two hours each, these films will inspire, disgust, move and encourage you. Watch these, please! They will forever change the way you approach and consider public education!

Documentaries:

IndoctriNation: Public Schools and the Decline of Christianity in America

The Cartel Movie – A Film by Bob Bowden

Expelled: No Intelligence Allowed

Agenda: Grinding America Down

Agenda 2: Masters of Deceit

Books:

Credentialed to Destroy: How and Why Education Became a Weapon, by Robin Eubanks

Dumbing Us Down: The Hidden Curriculum of Compulsory Schooling, 10th Anniversary Edition, by John Taylor Gatto

The Deliberate Dumbing Down of America, by Charlotte Iserbyt

Climbing Parnassus: A New Apologia for Greek and Latin, Tracy Lee Simmons

The Well-Trained Mind: A Guide to Classical Education at Home (Third Edition), by Susan Wise Bauer and Jessie Wise

The Story-Killers: A Common-Sense Case Against the Common Core, by Terrence O. Moore

Conform: Exposing the Truth About Common Core and Public Education, by Glenn Beck and Kyle Olson

The Long War on Common Core, by Donna Hearne

Other resources for beginning searches:

Classical Conversations (ClassicalConversations.com)
Carol Joy Seid (CarolJoySeid.com)
ConfessionsofaHomeschooler.com
Home School Legal Defense Association (HSLDA.org)
GreatHomeschoolConventions.com
Christian Home Educators Association of California (CHEAofCA.org)

Appendix

A letter to public school administrators.

Greetings of Peace,

On behalf of the Council on American-Islamic Relations (CAIR), please accept this gift of the Quran, Islam's revealed text, as an educational resource. In 2009, after President Obama's inspiring speech in Cairo promised a "new beginning" in America's relations with Muslims worldwide, CAIR launched the second phase of the *Explore the Quran* project, *Share the Quran*. Thus far, we have distributed over 100,000 copies to policymakers, media professionals, educators, as well as to public institutions and American citizens nationwide.

The wide media coverage and public support are a testament to the success of the project. The thank you letters and feedback we have received have let us know that the project has indeed been helpful in shedding light on the many misunderstandings about Islam that are prevalent today. We are now building on our past success and expanding this initiative to reach those in other segments of our society who share our commitment to mutual understanding.

The translator of this Quran, Leopold Weiss (1900-1992), who later adopted the name, Muhammad Asad, was an Austrian-Polish convert to Islam who had profound knowledge of the Judeo-Christian tradition. Asad ranks highly among the select group of well-known 20th century converts to Islam who subsequently took up scholarship. His translation and commentary is widely considered to be among the best in the English language. Moreover, his translation is complete with the original Arabic, English translation, commentary, historical notes and stunning examples of traditional Arabic calligraphy artwork. We have also included a bookmark that highlights some relevant issues of the day and verses from the Quran that address these issues.

Just a few helpful facts about the Quran:

- The Quran was revealed over 1400 years ago.
- Its revelation spanned the 23 year length of the Prophethood of Muhammad (peace be upon him) and addressed pertinent issues of the day which remain relevant even today.
- The Quran consists of 114 "surahs," typically translated as chapters."
- The Quran has been preserved word for word for centuries in its original Arabic language, is recited in the five daily prayers and millions of Muslims today have memorized it in its entirety.
- The Quran is believed by Muslims to be the final revealed scripture from God for the guidance of mankind. Other scriptures mentioned in the Quran that Muslims believe in include: the Psalms of David, the Torah of Moses, and the revelation sent to Jesus (peace be upon them).

We hope you will receive this in the spirit of interfaith cooperation and understanding in which it was intended and make it part of your reference library.

O men! Behold, We have created you all out of a male and a female, and have made you into nations and tribes, so that you might come to know one another. Verily, the noblest of you in the sight of God is the one who is most deeply conscious of Him. Behold, God is all-knowing, all-aware. Quran 49:13

Sincerely,

Nihad Awad
CAIR Executive Director

NOTES

[1] Geraghty, Jim. "Hillary and the NonFamily Enterprise of Education." The National Review. April 15, 2015. http://www.nationalreview.com/campaign-spot/416961/hillary-and-non-family-enterprise-education-jim-geraghty.
[2] James, Michael. "MSNBC: We Have To Break Through This Idea 'That Kids Belong to Their Parents.'" CNSNews. April 8, 2013. http://cnsnews.com/news/article/msnbc-we-have-break-through-idea-kids-belong-their-parents.
[3] Staff. "Number of Homeschoolers in US 2015-2016?" The A-to-Z of Homeschooling. Updated August 21,2015. http://a2zhomeschooling.com/thoughts_opinions_home_school/numbers_homeschooled_students/.
[4] Williamson, Kevin. "The Last Radicals." National Review Online. October 15, 2012. https://www.nationalreview.com/nrd/articles/328699/last-radicals.
[5] Reynolds, Dean. "Home Schoolers Lead Spelling Bee." ABC News. May 29, 2015. http://abcnews.go.com/WNT/story?id=130988.
[6] Rice, Mark. "Ranking America." January 6, 2015 & December 4, 2013. https://rankingamerica.wordpress.com/category/education/.
[7] Gatto, John Taylor. *The Underground History of American Education: A Schoolteacher's Intimate Investigation into the Problem of Modern Schooling*. Author's Special Pre-publication ed. New York: Oxford Village Press, 2000. https://archive.org/details/TheUndergroundHistoryOfAmericanEducation_758

[8] North, Gary. "Age-Grading is a Bad Idea". RonPaulHomeschooling.com. http://www.ronpaulhomeschooling.com/age-grading-is-a-bad-idea-gary-north/.

[9] https://swiftkickhq.com/top-15-steve-jobs-quotes-on-education/

[10] United States Department of State. THE U.S. AMBASSADORS FUND FOR CULTURAL PRESERVATION ANNUAL 05|06 REPORT." Implementation / The Department of State's Bureau of Educational and Cultural Affairs (ECA). https://eca.state.gov/files/bureau/2005-6afcpannual.pdf.

[11] Sheperd, Jessica. "World Education Rankings: which country does best at reading, maths and science?" The Guardian. December 7, 2010. http://www.guardian.co.uk/news/datablog/2010/dec/07/world-education-rankings-maths-science-reading.

[12] "Status Of the American Public School Teacher 2005–2006." National Education Association, NEA RESEARCH. March 1, 2010. Community and Civic Life / Political affiliation. http://www.unionfacts.com/downloads/Report_Status_of_American_Teachers_05_06.pdf.

[13] "UNIONFACTS.COM. USE OF DUES FOR POLITICS". Do Teachers Have a Lot to Learn? https://www.unionfacts.com/article/political-money/.

[14] "JammieWearingFool.": Another Union Success Story. January 31, 2010. http://jammiewearingfool.blogspot.com/2010/01/another-union-success-story.html.

[15] Cappell, Bill. "U.S. Students Slide In Global Ranking On Math, Reading, Science." - the two-way / BREAKING NEWS FROM NPR. December 3, 2013. http://www.npr.org/sections/thetwo-way/2013/12/03/248329823/u-s-high-school-students-slide-in-math-reading-science.

[16] Chappell, Bill. "US High School Students Slide in Math, Reading, Science." - the two-way / BREAKING NEWS FROM

NPR. December 3, 2013. http://www.scpr.org/news/2013/12/03/40715/us-high-school-students-slide-in-math-reading-scie/.

[1717] Noguchi, Sharon. "California Graduation Rates Rise; so Do Dropout Rates." San Jose Mercury News. April 29, 2015. http://www.mercurynews.com/bay-area-news/ci_28006935/graduation-rates-rise-so-do-dropout-rates.

[18] "11 Facts About High School Dropout Rates." DoingSomething.org. https://www.dosomething.org/facts/11-facts-about-high-school-dropout-rates.

[19]http://www.brainyquote.com/quotes/quotes/t/theodorero147900.html

[20] Hill, Austin. "Common Core And The All-Too-Common Tendencies Of Heavy-Handed Government." Townhall.com. May 5, 2013. http://townhall.com/columnists/austinhill/2013/05/05/common-core-and-the-alltoocommon-tendencies-of-heavyhanded-government-n1587366/page/full.

[21] Clark, Austin. "A Timeline of Major American Education Reform Since 1958." Racing to the Top. January 14, 2010. http://austinclark4.wordpress.com/2010/01/14/a-timeline-of-major-american-education-reform-since-1958/.

[22] Opelka, Mike, "NY's Common Core-Aligned Lessons Use Scientology Videos to Teach Students They Have Right to Food, Housing, Clothing, Medicine, Even a Job". The Blaze. March 30, 2013. http://www.theblaze.com/stories/2013/03/30/common-core-uses-scientology-videos-to-teach-students-they-have-right-to-food-housing-clothing-medicine-even-a-job/.

[23] Source adapted from Pam Costain, Moving the Agenda Forward, Connection to the Americas 14.8 (October 1997):4.

[24] "Universal Declaration of Human Rights – Article 16". http://www.un.org/en/universal-declaration-human-rights/.

[25] "Universal Declaration of Human Rights – Article 25". http://www.un.org/en/universal-declaration-human-rights/.

---

26 Merriam-Webster. http://www.merriam-webster.com/dictionary/slavery.
27 Velderman, Ben. "Fifth-grader Receives Credit for Claiming Human Rights Are Gifts of Government." EAGnews.org. October 2, 2013. http://eagnews.org/elementary-student-receives-credit-for-declaring-that-human-rights-are-gifts-of-government/.
28 Dalberg-Acton, John, 1st Baron Acton. http://www.acton.org/research/lord-acton-quote-archive.
29 Http://Goodreads.com/author/show/1244.Mark_Twain
30 Reil, William Taylor. "More about Common Core." Times News, LLC. June 8, 2013. http://www.tnonline.com/2013/jun/08/more-about-common-core.
31 "Standards in Your State." Common Core State Standards Initiative. 2015. Common Core State Standards Initiative. http://www.corestandards.org/standards-in-your-state/.
32 Stotsky, Sandra. "Sandra Stotsky on the ELA Common Core Standards." Utahns Against Common Core. July 17, 2012. http://www.utahnsagainstcommoncore.com/sandra-stotsky-on-the-ela-common-core-standards/.
33 Krieger, Larry. "29 Biased Statements In the AP U.S. History Redesign." The Heartland Institute. August 19, 2014. http://news.heartland.org/newspaper-article/2014/08/19/29-biased-statements-ap-us-history-redesign.
34 Wood, Peter. "The New AP History: A Preliminary Report." National Association of Scholars. July 1, 2014. https://www.nas.org/articles/the_new_ap_history_a_preliminary_report.
35 Robbins, Jane, and Larry Krieger. "New Advanced Placement Framework Distorts America's History." The Heartland Institute. March 26, 2014. http://news.heartland.org/newspaper-article/2014/03/26/new-advanced-placement-framework-distorts-americas-history.

---

[36] Krieger, Larry. "Yes, the New AP Framework Does Distort U.S. History." The Heartland Institute. April 9, 2014. http://news.heartland.org/newspaper-article/2014/04/09/yes-new-ap-framework-does-distort-us-history.
[37] AP Advances in AP.Statement on AP U.S. History. September 19, 2014 https://advancesinap.collegeboard.org/english-history-and-social-science/us-history/college-board-statement.
[38] Byrne, Kevin B., Edward M. Dickson, Jr., Jason George, Geraldine Ann Hastings Hastings, John P. Irish, Emma Jones Lapsansky-Werner, Cassandra A. Osborne, Suzanne M. Sinke, and Timothy N. Thurber. "An Open Letter from the Authors of the AP United States History Curriculum Framework." Education Week. August, 2014. http://www.edweek.org/media/letter-us-history.pdf.
[39] Henninger, Daniel. "Hey, Conservatives, You Won." WSJ. August 26, 2015. http://www.wsj.com/articles/hey-conservatives-you-won-1440628311.
[40] "Resolution Concerning Advanced Placement." Accessed 2015. http://blogs.edweek.org/edweek/curriculum/RNC.JPG.
[41] Conlon, Kevin. "Oklahoma Bill Would Make AP U.S. History history - CNN.com." CNN. Updated February 19, 2015. http://www.cnn.com/2015/02/18/us/oklahoma-ap-history/.
[42] Howerton, Jason. "Wait Until You See How a High School Textbook Summarizes the Rights Guaranteed in the Second Amendment." The Blaze. September 16, 2013. http://www.theblaze.com/stories/2013/09/16/wait-until-you-see-how-a-high-school-textbook-summarizes-the-rights-granted-in-the-second-amendment/.
[43] Ahlert, Arnold. "Saddam's WMDs: The Left's Iraq Lies Exposed." Frontpage Mag. June 22, 2014. http://www.frontpagemag.com/fpm/234626/saddams-wmds-lefts-iraq-lies-exposed-arnold-ahlert.
[44] Howerton, Jason. "Wait Until You See How a High School Textbook Summarizes the Rights Guaranteed in the Second

Amendment." The Blaze. September 16, 2013. http://www.theblaze.com/stories/2013/09/16/wait-until-you-see-how-a-high-school-textbook-summarizes-the-rights-granted-in-the-second-amendment/.

[45] BlackPast.org. "The Deleted Passage of the Declaration of Independence (1776) ..." http://www.blackpast.org/primary/declaration-independence-and-debate-over-slavery#sthash.Brr3254y.dpuf.

[46] Datoc, Christian. "Sanders: America Was Founded On 'Racist Principles. That's A Fact.'." The DC. September 14, 2015. http://dailycaller.com/2015/09/14/sanders-america-was-founded-on-racist-principles-thats-a-fact-video/ - ixzz3mC4eQy3t.

[47] Opelka, Mike. "NY's Common Core-Aligned Lessons Use Scientology Videos to Teach Students They Have Right to Food, Housing, Clothing, Medicine, Even a Job." The Blaze. March 30, 2013. Accessed January 18, 2016. http://www.theblaze.com/stories/2013/03/30/common-core-uses-scientology-videos-to-teach-students-they-have-right-to-food-housing-clothing-medicine-even-a-job/.

[48] Missouri Education Watchdog : Watching the DESE Countdown Clock. "Citizens Still Waiting for Answers to Questions from the May 2 Hearings." Before It's News. March 15, 2013. http://missourieducationwatchdog.blogspot.com/2013/05/watching-dese-countdown-clock-citizens.html.

[49] Bollman, Brian. "Search Results for 'Common Core May 2, 2013'." The Rockin Conservative. May 02, 2013. Accessed January 18, 2016. http://rockinconservative.com/?s=Common Core May 2, 2013.

[50]http://tcfir.org/opinion/Thomas%20Jefferson%20on%20Educating%20the%20People.pdf

[51] Soave, Robby. "Here's What Kids Will Read under Common Core." May 8, 2013.

http://dailycaller.com/2013/05/08/heres-what-kids-will-read-under-common-core/.
[52]http://www.brainyquote.com/quotes/quotes/a/aristotle100584.html
[53] Schneider, Mercedes. "My First Days With Full-blown Common Core." deutsch29. August 08, 2013. https://deutsch29.wordpress.com/2013/08/08/my-first-days-with-full-blown-common-core/.
[54] Schneider, Mercedes. "My First Days With Full-blown Common Core." deutsch29. August 08, 2013. https://deutsch29.wordpress.com/2013/08/08/my-first-days-with-full-blown-common-core/.
[55]http://www.brainyquote.com/quotes/quotes/r/robertfros101423.html
[56] Hennessy, Matthew. "Homeschooling in the City." City Journal, Summer 2015. http://www.city-journal.org/2015/25_3_homeschooling.html.
[57] Silver, James. "Classroom Disruptor: the Proprietary Tablet PC That's Changing Russian Schools (Wired UK)." Wired UK.CO.UK." February 24, 2012. http://www.wired.co.uk/magazine/archive/2012/03/features/classroom-disruptor.
[58]http://www.brainyquote.com/quotes/quotes/b/benjaminfr383997.html
[59] "Fiscal Year 2012, Budget of the U.S. Government." Budget Documents. https://www.whitehouse.gov/sites/default/files/omb/budget/fy2012/assets/education.pdf.
[60] Burke, Henry. "State-Specific Common Core Implementation Costs." Education News. February 19, 2015. http://www.educationviews.org/state-specific-common-core-implementation-costs-2/.
[61] Chiaramonte, Perry. "High Cost of Common Core has states rethinking the national education standards | Fox News." Fox News. February 05, 2014. http://www.foxnews.com/us/2014/02/05/number-states-

backing-out-common-core-testing-maryland-schools-low-on-funding/.
[62] Estrada, William A. "Paul Ryan: Keep Homeschooling Free!" HSLDA. October 22, 2012. http://www.hslda.org/docs/news/2012/201210220.asp.
[63] James, Michael. "MSNBC: We Have to Break Through This Idea 'That Kids Belong to Their Parents'. cnsnews.com. April 8, 2013. http://cnsnews.com/news/article/msnbc-we-have-break-through-idea-kids-belong-their-parents.
[64] Farris, Michael P. "HSLDA | Newborn Seized in Hospital by Police, Social Worker." HSLDA | Newborn Seized in Hospital by Police, Social Worker. March 27, 2012. https://www.hslda.org/hs/state/pa/201203270.asp.
[65] Hanchett, Ian. "EPA Head McCarthy: Even If We Lose Suit, We Pretty Much Got Regs to Work Anyway." Breitbart News. June 26, 2015. http://www.breitbart.com/video/2015/06/26/epa-head-mccarthy-even-if-we-lose-suit-we-pretty-much-got-regs-to-work-anyway/.
[66] http://www.john-adams-heritage.com/quotes/
[67] "Parents Alarmed By 'Pleasure Activists' in High School Classroom'." Pacific Justice Institute. January 14, 2015. http://www.pacificjustice.org/press-releases/parents-alarmed-by-pleasure-activist-in-high-school-classroom.
[68] Samuel, Stephanie. "Planned Parenthood Distributes 'Genderbread Person' Sex-Ed Leaflet in Schools; Teaches Students They Can Be 'Genderqueer,' 'Genderless' 'Two-Spirit'" Christian Post US. December 12, 2014. http://www.christianpost.com/news/planned-parenthood-distributes-genderbread-person-sex-ed-leaflet-at-school-teaches-students-they-can-be-genderqueer-genderless-two-spirit-131115/.
[69] Swank, Greg. "The Communist Takeover Of America - 45 Declared Goals." The Communist Takeover Of America - 45 Declared Goals. April 2, 2012. http://www.rense.com/general32/americ.htm.

---

[70] Russell, Bertrand. "Bertrand Russell Securesites."Quotes and Excerpts by file://localhost/Bertrand Russell. http/::kjos1.securesites.net:Quotes:fascism:Bertrand Russell.htm.

[71] Wikipedia. "Education – Wikipedia, the free encyclopedia". https://en.wikipedia.org/wiki/Education.

[72] Swank, Greg. "The Communist Takeover Of America - 45 Declared Goals." file://localhost/Rense.com. April 2, 2012. http/::rense.com:general32:americ.htm.

[73] "Sam Sorbo." "video - Kevin and Sam Sorbo Part 1 and Part 2." TheBlaze TV. http://www.video.theblaze.com/video/topic/66364238/v31405007/sam-sorbo.

[74] Simmons, Tracey Lee. *Climbing Parnassus: a new apologia for Greek and Latin.* Wilmington, DE: ISI, 2002. 3-5. Print.

[75] http://www.nsa.edu/t-s-eliot-on-liberal-education/

[76] Chapman, Ben, and Brown, Stephen Rex. "Michael Mulgrew Defends Common Core: 'you sick people need to deal with us'." NY Daily News. August 8, 2014. http://www.nydailynews.com/new-york/education/michael-mulgrew-defends-common-core-punch-face-tools-article-1.1895301.

[77] Brown, Lauretta. "Student Attacks on Teachers Up 34.5%; Record 209,800 in 2011-12 School Year." CNSNews. June 10, 2014. http://www.cnsnews.com/news/article/lauretta-brown/student-attacks-teachers-345-record-209800-2011-12-school-year

[78] Harmon, Katherine. "Contact with Your Infant?" Scientific American. May 6, 2010. http://www.scientificamerican.com/article/infant-touch/

[79] Breen, Audrey. "Study: States' Methods for Rating Preschool Quality Fail to Predict Children's Readiness for Kindergarten." UVA Today. August 22, 2013. https://news.virginia.edu/content/study-states-methods-rating-preschool-quality-fail-predict-children-s-readiness-kindergarten.

[80] Courtney, Jennifer. "Can Books Really Teach Us Anything? (Part One)." Classical Conversations. July 9, 2013. https://www.classicalconversations.com/article/can-books-really-teach-us-anything-part-one.
[81] President Adams, John Quotes. "John Adams Quotes." BrainyQuote.com http://www.brainyquote.com/quotes/quotes/j/johnadams391045.html
[82] "Arizona School Forcing All Female Students To Wear Hijab For One Month." National Report RSS. February 03, 2015. http://nationalreport.net/arizona-school-forcing-female-students-wear-hijab-one-month/.
[83] Starnes, Todd. "'There Is No God but Allah'? School Accused of Islamic Indoctrination." Fox News Opinion. September 10, 2015. http://www.foxnews.com/opinion/2015/09/10/there-is-no-god-but-allah-school-accused-islamic-indoctrination.html.
[84] Chumley, Cheryl. "Michigan School Tells 10th-Graders to Design Islamic Pamphlet for Third-Graders. The Washington Times. October 7, 2014. http://www.washingtontimes.com/news/2014/oct/7/michigan-school-tells-10th-graders-to-design-islam/.
[85] Merritt, Jonathan. "Why Conservative Christians Should Oppose Teaching the Bible in Public Schools - On Faith and Culture." Religion News Service [RNS]. March 04, 2013. http://jonathanmerritt.religionnews.com/2013/03/04/why-conservative-christians-should-oppose-teaching-the-bible-in-public-school/.
[86] Downey, Roma and Burnett, Mark. "Why Public Schools Should Teach the Bible." The Wall Street Journal. March 1, 2013. http://www.wsj.com/articles/SB10001424127887324338604578326150289837608
[87] Bible Literacy Project. http://www.bibleliteracy.org

About the Author

Sam Sorbo hosts the nationally syndicated Sam Sorbo Show, weekdays. After high school in Pittsburgh, PA, Sam (Jenkins) Sorbo studied biomedical engineering at Duke University before pursuing a career in modeling. Modeling offered the opportunity to travel and learn languages; she is fluent in five. Sam moved to Los Angeles for acting, where dedication and perseverance gained her roles in several films, including *Bonfire of the Vanities* and *Twenty Bucks*, and TV shows, including *Chicago Hope* and *Hercules: The Legendary Journeys.* As Guest Star on *Hercules* she met Kevin Sorbo, who swept her off her feet. They married in 1998 and she moved to New Zealand. While living in Auckland, Sam created and published a humorous and educational photo-book, Gizmoe: The Legendary Journeys, Auckland. Her second book, co-authored with Marius Forté, is The Answer: Proof of God in Heaven. In addition to her radio show, Sam continues to perform in movies: *Hope Bridge, Storm Rider,* and for her role in *Just Let Go* she won Best Supporting Actress from the Utah Film Awards. In 2016 Sam created *Miracle Man,* a television show produced by NBC and Sony, and the Sorbos are currently in production on several films. They home school their three children.

www.SamSorbo.com

Facebook.com/SamSorbo

@TheSamSorboShow

Reveille Press

52016459R00125

Made in the USA
Lexington, KY
13 May 2016